AMERICA HELD HOSTAGE

DON LAWSON

AMERICA
HELD HOSTAGE
THE IRAN HOSTAGE CRISIS AND
THE IRAN-CONTRA AFFAIR

FOREWORD BY
ARTHUR L. LIMAN

BARBARA SILBERDICK FEINBERG,
CONSULTING EDITOR

A TWENTIETH CENTURY
AMERICAN HISTORY BOOK
FRANKLIN WATTS
NEW YORK LONDON TORONTO SYDNEY
1991

Library of Congress Cataloging-in-Publication Data

Lawson, Don.
America held hostage : the Iran hostage crisis and the Iran-contra
affair / Don Lawson : foreword by Arthur L. Liman : Barbara
Silberdick Feinberg, consulting editor.
p.   cm. — (A Twentieth century American history book)
Includes bibliographical references and index.
Summary: Describes how extremist groups and governments have
resorted to hostage taking in recent years, and shows how both the
Carter and Reagan administration have dealt with such crises.
ISBN 0-531-11009-5
1. Iran Hostage Crisis, 1979–1981.   2. Iran-Contra Affair,
1985–1990. [1. Iran Hostage Crisis, 1979–1981.   2. Iran-Contra
Affair, 1985–1990.   3. Hostages.]   I. Feinberg, Barbara Silberdick.
II. Title.   III. Series.
E183.I55L38   1991
973.926—dc20   90-20515   CIP   AC

CONTENTS

AMERICA HELD HOSTAGE

FOREWORD

The Iran-Contra affair mesmerized the world in 1987. Literally hundreds of millions of people watched Oliver North and other witnesses appear before the Congressional hearings in the summer of 1987. Why did the Iran-Contra affair so engage the attention of the public? What is its true meaning and what lessons can we derive for the future?

On one level, the Iran-Contra affair was an epic foreign policy fiasco, not the first nor the last in our history. We had two contradictory foreign policies—one public and one secret; one known by the Congress, the Cabinet, and the American people, and the other known only by a few in the White House, plus (ironically) an assortment of shadowy international arms merchants, Iranian terrorists, and Nicaraguan Sandinistas.

Publicly, the United States had vowed not to negotiate with terrorists or pay ransom for hostages. The then-vice-president, George Bush, had headed a presidential commission that as recently as 1986 had reaffirmed this policy, saying that to capitulate to terrorists was to invite more hostage-taking. The United States had also adopted an arms embargo against Iran, which in 1979 had humiliated the United States by seizing the United States embassy in Iran and which was engaged in a war with Iraq. The State Department, in fact, chastised other countries for breaking the arms embargo by selling military equipment to Iran. Finally, the United States—after first supporting insurgents (known as the Contras) opposed to the Marxist Sandinista regime in Nicaragua—had adopted a policy, embodied in legislation, that barred the United States government from funding military support to the Contras. The president publicly declared that he would comply with this law, even though he was a firm supporter of the Contra forces.

In the Iran-Contra affair, all three of these public policies were violated by the president or his aides. Despite the arms embargo, the president clandestinely sold sophisticated missiles to Iran. He did so to get American hostages back despite the policy against concessions to hostage-takers. Some hostages were, in fact, released in return for the arms; but once the terrorists were aware that the United States was willing to supply arms for hostages, more Americans were kidnapped, one for each hostage who was released. The vicious cycle of more arms for hostages could have continued uninterrupted for years had not a Lebanese newspaper exposed the covert arms sales in November 1986. By then, the Iranian negotiators were demanding even more sophisticated missiles, and the president was considering providing them in return for the release of American hostages. All of this occurred behind a veil of secrecy. The American people knew nothing of it, the Congress knew nothing of it; even Cabinet officers, like the secretary of state and the secretary of defense who protested the arms sales to Iran, were cut off from information.

What is worse, the arms were sold to Iran at a huge profit, which was then diverted for other improper purposes. A part of the profits was used to buy arms for the

Contras, the very military assistance which United States law forbade. Most of the rest was used to create a secret network of corporations, called the Enterprise, run by Oliver North and his associate, retired General Richard Secord, to engage in covert operations designed to undermine communist or unfriendly governments throughout the world. The Enterprise, operating outside the control of responsible government officials and accountable to no government institution, could engage in para-military and other covert activities in which the CIA was barred from engaging by law. The Enterprise had airplanes, secret communications devices, Swiss bank accounts, and grandiose plans. The Enterprise was more like an invention in a James Bond movie than the product of a constitutional democracy.

Deception permeated the whole Iran-Contra affair. But the deception was not aimed at our enemies. Iran, and the terrorists who held the American hostages, knew that the president was selling arms to Iran for their release; and the government in Nicaragua was aware that we were continuing to arm the Contras. The deception in the Iran-Contra affair was aimed at Congress, the responsible cabinet officers, and the American people. Indeed, even the chairman of the Joint Chiefs of Staff was not entrusted with all of the information about the activities of Colonel North and his associates.

To cover their tracks, participants in the Iran-Contra affair lied when Congress began asking questions. (Colonel North was convicted of obstructing Congress; and a former National Security Adviser, Robert C. McFarlane, and retired General Secord pled guilty to charges of a similar nature.) North and Rear Admiral John M. Poindexter, who served as National Security Adviser after McFarlane, also shredded and altered documents so that the truth would not be revealed. Thus, for the second time in a generation—the first being Watergate—presidential aides engaged in a cover-up.

The real significance, however, of the Iran-Contra affair is not, I submit, the specific acts of wrongdoing, or even the damage done abroad to America's reputation for openness. Rather, the most ominous aspect of the affair was the disrespect, bordering on contempt, for constitutional safeguards and the rule of law demonstrated by the participants. Colonel North's secretary, Fawn Hall, summed up the attitude best when she testified that "sometimes one has to rise above the written law."

United States laws that had banned military aid to the Contras and required that Congress be notified of arms sales were seen by the president's aides as obstacles that stood in the way of accomplishing their goals. They therefore felt morally justified in disregarding these laws. All of those who watched the Iran-Contra hearings will remember Oliver North's impassioned defense of lying to Congress. To him, the end—supporting the Contras, or seeking to advance the president's goal of releasing the hostages—justified virtually all the means.

With Colonel North and Admiral Poindexter championing the doctrine of presidential prerogatives, the Iran-Contra hearings reignited a debate that took place 200 years ago when our Constitution was adopted. At that time, there were delegates to the Constitutional Convention who believed that a president should have powers almost equivalent to that of a king, and who despised a democratically elected legislature, which they thought might pander to the shifting opinions of the public. But the prevailing view at the Constitutional Convention was mistrust of governmental power. The majority of the delegates refused to concentrate power in any one branch. They therefore created a separation and division of powers with sufficient checks and balances to protect the public against the arrogance or misadministration of anyone. It is no accident of drafting that while the Constitution makes the president the commander in chief of the armed forces, it gives Congress alone the power to declare war or to raise armies or maintain navies. Nor was it an accident that the president, despite his role as the architect of foreign policy, is required by the Constitution to seek Senate ratification of any treaty and cannot spend money unless it is appropriated by the Congress. Dictatorships, not democracies, have one-person rule. Dictatorships, not democracies, are therefore now crumbling throughout the world.

Our Constitution was designed to safeguard the people by diffusing power, by requiring the branches to cooperate with one another and by enshrining the rule of law. Every year at its commencement, the president of Harvard University in awarding law degrees describes law as the "wise restraints that make men free." This is precisely the philosophy underlying the United States Constitution.

The participants in the Iran-Contra affair ignored—and violated—this fundamental precept of American democracy. They were frustrated that the Congress, supported by the American people, was not prepared to become involved in another Vietnam, this time in Nicaragua. They were frustrated that they could not get the hostages back, and that the president's power to sell arms for hostages was limited by legal requirements of notification to Congress. They even belittled the CIA because, as an established institution of government, it was accountable to Congress and governed by law. So they chose to circumvent constitutional processes, to create outside of the government an enterprise that could do what the government was prohibited from doing, and then to lie about it. They created, in a short time, a secret government within the government. And *that* is the story of Iran-Contra.

President Reagan's role in the Iran-Contra affair remains unresolved. The president made the decision to sell arms to Iran against the advice of his secretaries of state and defense. He made the decision to keep the sales secret from Congress and from the public. He also made the decision to have the National Security Council staff continue to lend support to the Contras. But the president has been insistent that he did not know of the diversion and never authorized any of his aides to lie to Congress, to shred or alter documents requested by Congress, or to violate the law. The Senate and House Committees, in their majority report, concluded that even if the president was not involved in these activities, he bears the ultimate responsibility, for he "created or at least tolerated an environment" in which those who caused the diversion, evaded the Boland Amendment and engaged in the coverup, "believed with certainty that they were carrying out the President's policies." As Admiral Poindexter, the president's National Security Adviser, put it concerning aid to the Contras, "Frankly, we were willing to take some risks with the law." That is an intolerable attitude. In a constitutional democracy, ends cannot justify the means, and the Constitution requires the president to "take care that the laws be faithfully executed, whether or not he agrees with the law." Schemes to get around the law violate this fundamental command.

In the end, the Iran-Contra affair backfired on its participants. The tradition of the rule of law and democracy is too great in this country to tolerate escapades like Iran-Contra. The Iran-Contra affair was not only exposed but examined in minute detail in televised hearings in full public view. And so, when we lament the folly and lawlessness that the Iran-Contra affair represented, we should also praise the American spirit of openness and accountability that, in the end, could not be suppressed and that was illustrated by the public hearings Congress held. When other countries have foreign policy debacles, they hush them up or conduct their inquiries behind closed doors. We, however, were willing to expose the indiscretions even of a popular president for the whole world to see. By so doing, we showed the strength of our democracy.

Many years ago, Justice Louis Brandeis, one of our greatest jurists, wrote that in a democracy "sunlight is the best disinfectant." That is what I believe to be the most enduring lesson of the Iran-Contra affair and one that is worth transmitting to our young people in books like this. Open government is the American tradition. The Iran-Contra affair was an aberration.

Arthur L. Liman

NOTE: Arthur L. Liman was the Chief Counsel of the United States Senate Select Committee on Secret Military Assistance to Iran and the Nicaraguan Opposition. He was not involved in the preparation of this book and bears no responsibility for its contents. The views in this foreword are his own.

"NEST OF SPIES"

The American embassy in Tehran, the capital of the country of Iran, was not situated in the same section of the city as the embassies of other nations. The embassies of Great Britain, the Soviet Union, Germany, and others, were impressive buildings on Ferdowski Avenue. They were surrounded by thick brick walls ten to twelve feet high. The American embassy was situated on Takht Jamskid Street, which, up until relatively recently, had been paved with cobblestones. It occupied several plain buildings whose grounds were easily accessible to passersby. When the American embassy had first been established there in the 1940s, its grounds were surrounded by a low wooden fence. Now this fence had been replaced by an equally low iron fence that did little to keep out possible trespassers. Immediately facing the street, however, was a small area of fence made of concrete. It was this fence that would be pictured in most television news shots.

In the beginning the Iranian people highly approved of the message that the United States seemed to be sending out with its easily accessible embassy: America wanted to be divorced from the other world powers that had kept Iran under their thumbs for more than a century. America wanted to be Iran's friend and would approach the Iranians on a warm, person-to-person basis. But by the autumn of 1979, this friendly atmosphere between local Iranians and the Americans housed in the embassy had completely vanished. Now the Iranians held daily demonstrations in front of the American embassy. Most of the demonstrators were students, many of whom had studied in the United States. These students, who had once proudly proclaimed their friendship with America and the Americans, now carried placards that read: Down with the American Satan, Americans Go Home, Death to the Shah. The embassy itself must be wiped out, the students insisted, because it was nothing more than "a nest of spies."

Anti-Americanism in Iran had grown out of the United States' support of Iran's longtime leader, Shah Mohammed Reza Pahlavi. The Shah's reign had been dictatorial and oppressive, and in the late 1970s Iranian Muslim revolutionaries rebelled against it. Driven out of the country, the Shah subsequently sought asylum in the United States. The Iranian revolutionaries warned the United States against granting such asylum. Fearing retaliation, the United States was at first reluctant to allow the Shah to enter, but soon it became generally known that he was suffering from cancer. In late October 1979, U.S. President Jimmy Carter gave permission for the Shah to be admitted to the country for treatment at a New York City hospital. Demonstrations outside the U.S. embassy in Tehran immediately reached a fever pitch.

So far as is known the takeover of the American embassy was not planned. On Sunday morning, November 4, several Iranian student demonstrators simply drifted inside the grounds. When they met no physical resistance they encouraged other demonstrators to join them. Soon forty or fifty young Iranian militants were roaming through the compound and up and down the embassy halls. At this point the several U.S. Marines who were on guard duty tried to eject the intruders. When they refused to leave, the Marines sounded an alarm throughout the embassy. But by now the demonstrators had decided to stage a sit-in. Several of the students who had studied in the United States had seen how effective sit-ins could be in emphasizing demonstrators' demands at American universities. They decided to use the same technique.

The occupation of the American embassy by the Iranians immediately brought American television crews and reporters to the scene. To them the students announced that they planned to stage a continuous sit-in until the Shah and his multimillion-dollar fortune were returned to Iran. They also said they planned on holding everyone in the embassy as hostages until their demands were met. At this time there were about a hundred American diplomats and Iranian employees in the embassy, but the occupying force of students had swollen to several hundred so there was little doubt that the demonstrators could carry out their plan.

News of the embassy takeover caused an instant sensation in the United States. Television newscasts were filled with on-the-scene pictures of the dramatic event which was virtually unprecedented in American history. Everywhere the American public demanded that the government take some sort of retaliatory action. Even other nations such as France and Great Britain expressed their strong disapproval of the Iranian action.

The only concession the demonstrators made was to release all of the non-American hostages as well as all of the blacks and most of the women. The blacks were released, the Muslims said, because they were victims of the white American oppressors. The women were freed because Muslims did not wage war against women.

During this period of early confusion six Americans,

four men and two women, escaped from the embassy by simply walking out and making their way to the Canadian embassy. There they were allowed to take refuge for several months before they were given false Canadian passports and flown to Canada and then the United States. The number of hostages was finally pared down to fifty-two, but these people would be held, their captors claimed, until all Muslim demands were met. In the United States, the cry for retaliatory action grew louder.

Americans were angered over their fellow citizens being taken hostage because of the basic American belief in human freedom and individual rights. This belief was built into the U.S. Constitution and the Bill of Rights, and whenever it was challenged by a foreign power or powers, the American people expected their government to strike back in defense of it. The American Revolution had been fought to establish this principle in law, and from time to time since then it had been stoutly defended.

An incident somewhat similar to the Iran hostage situation had occurred in the eighteenth and nineteenth centuries when Barbary pirates along the northern coast of Africa captured American seamen sailing in the Mediterranean Sea and held them for ransom. By the time Thomas Jefferson became president in 1801, the United States had paid out some $2 million in ransom money. Jefferson put an end to that practice by building up the U.S. Navy and going to war against the pirates, forcing them to sue for peace and end their piratical ways. Since then the rights and personal freedom of every American traveling abroad had been assumed as part of the responsibility of the United States government.

Foreign nations as well as the United States were angered over Iran's hostage-taking activity, mainly because it violated the long-accepted rule that embassies on another nation's soil were totally private and not to be entered without permission from the country they represented. In other words, an embassy was like a private piece of one country placed within another country's borders. This so-called "embassy and diplomatic immunity" even went so far as to make a foreign nation's diplomats immune to the laws of the country in which their embassy was located.

Another aspect of embassy and diplomatic immunity was that occasionally, local law breakers—often political dissidents—would enter a foreign embassy and seek refuge there. This had occurred several times in American embassies where political prisoners escaped their captors and sought refuge with the Americans. Such refuge had become a part of widely accepted international law, but now the Iranians had violated this law by boldly taking over the American embassy in Tehran.

The one person who could have brought this hostage situation to a quick halt was the Ayatollah Ruhollah Khomeini, who had returned from fifteen years in exile to take over the Iranian government when the Shah fled. But as a leader of the Muslim revolutionaries (*ayatollah* means a religious leader in the Shia or Shiite branch of the Islamic religion), Khomeini was not in the least interested in accommodating what he regarded as the godless Western world. A religious fanatic, Khomeini was only interested in the downfall of the "Great Satan," as he dubbed the United States, and in the worldwide spread of his particular branch of Islamic beliefs.

What Khomeini did do was to approve of the students' actions by sending his son Ahmad to congratulate them on their "splendid Islamic act." When reporters asked Khomeini if he wasn't fearful of U.S. reaction, the Ayatollah responded, "America cannot do a damned thing."[1] And, frustrating as it was, this assessment of the situation apparently proved to be all too true.

Day after day the Iranian militants demonstrated in front of the American embassy. They burned American flags, shouted obscene insults at the world in general and the United States in particular, and continued to demand the return of the Shah. Iranians from throughout the country made special trips to Tehran just to join in the spectacle of humbling America and the Americans. Tourist travel increased when Islamic religious leaders told their followers that a trip to the besieged American embassy in Tehran could be substituted for a trip to Mecca, the Muslim holy city in Saudi Arabia to which all Muslims are supposed to make a pilgrimage before they die.

Inside the embassy the student revolutionaries studied captured documents and learned that several U.S. "diplomats" had actually been Central Intelligence Agency (CIA) members. The CIA uses undercover agents or spies to gather secret information about foreign governments and their activities. Although it had long been common knowledge among all of the world's diplomats that all nations used their embassies as cover for a few intelligence agents, the militant students did not know this and announced that the embassy had been nothing less than a "nest of spies." This further infuriated the Iranians demonstrating outside the embassy.

Back in the United States, President Carter continued to seek some way out of the hostage situation. He sent various high-ranking political figures to Tehran, but they were only laughed at and insulted. Carter then stopped the shipment of all military matériel that the United States had planned to export to Iran. Later he declared a full economic ban on all goods to Iran. He also ordered that all Iranian money and assets in American banks (twelve billion dollars' worth) be frozen. Finally, when all these measures produced no positive results, the United States broke all relations with Iran.

In what proved to be a highly controversial move, Carter also ordered that all of the estimated 50,000 Iranian students studying in the United States had to be re-registered. Any found to be in violation of any immigration regulations were to be deported. But the paperwork involved in this effort proved to be too much for the government bureaucrats to handle, so the move was quietly dropped.

Actually neither any of the Carter administration's efforts nor attempts by other countries to intercede on behalf of the United States had any effect. The Iran hostage stalemate continued. Finally, believing he had exhausted all diplomatic efforts in the hostages' behalf, President Carter decided to send in a military mission to rescue them.

Carter, like a number of other leading statesmen, had been greatly impressed with a rescue mission performed by Israeli commandos in 1976. It had been a model for such rescue efforts ever since.

In May 1976, an Air France airliner had been hijacked by unidentified terrorists at the Athens airport in Greece. From Athens the plane had been forced to fly to Entebbe, Uganda, in northern Africa. Among the passengers were some 102 Jews, most of whom had boarded the aircraft at Tel Aviv in Israel. The captives were held at the Entebbe airport for more than a week while Israel apparently negotiated for their release in exchange for anti-Israel terrorists who had been captured earlier by the Israelis.

But actually the Israelis had no intention of negotiating a prisoner exchange. They were determined to teach Idi Amin, the anti-Semitic leader of Uganda, a lesson. Idi Amin had been issuing anti-Semitic statements including one in praise of Adolf Hitler and his treatment of the Jews in World War II, and the Israelis were not in the habit of letting such insults pass without retaliation. They retaliated with a daring rescue mission at Entebbe. While negotiations were apparently going on, a team of Israeli commandos (special troops trained to raid and operate inside enemy territory) secretly flew the 2,500 miles from Israel to Uganda, landing in the middle of the night. The Israelis quietly invaded the compound in which the hostages were held, killed half a dozen terrorist guards, and escaped safely back to Israel with all of the Israeli prisoners as well as the Air France crew. All the hostages survived the rescue unharmed. The raid had been carried out with such surgical precision that Idi Amin did not know until the next morning what had happened.

Now President Carter planned to mount an Entebbe-like raid on Tehran. Because the raid would be so risky, Secretary of State Cyrus Vance was strongly opposed to it. Vance, in fact, feared that it might even lead to war with Iran. Nevertheless, Carter and his aides went ahead with it.

The top secret mission was called Eagle Claw. Intended as a bold air-land-sea rescue operation, it ended in disaster shortly after it started. Eagle Claw was headed by Colonel Charles Beckwith, a veteran special forces officer. The special forces command under Beckwith for this mission was called Delta Force, a unit specially trained for just such a rescue situation. Delta Force was made up of about 200 men, half of them U.S. Army commandos.

Operation Eagle Claw began at about dawn on April 24, 1980, when eight Sea Stallion helicopters were launched from the U.S. aircraft carrier *Nimitz* sailing in the Arabian Sea off the southeast coast of Iran. At the same time six Hercules transport aircraft took off from an undisclosed location for a rendezvous with the helicopters at a place in the Iranian desert called Desert One, several hundred miles southeast of Tehran. From Desert One the combined rescue team was supposed to fly to Desert Two.

There the raiders were to board trucks for a further 50-mile trip into Tehran. In Tehran the raiders were to hide briefly in Amjadieh Stadium near the U.S. embassy. At the stadium and elsewhere along the way they were to be aided by several Iranians who were sympathetic to the United States and who had been hired by the CIA.

The raiders were then to storm the American embassy, kill whoever tried to stop them, free the hostages, and bring them to the stadium where the helicopters would by then be on hand to carry the freed prisoners to Desert One. At Desert One the freed prisoners would be flown out of the country on board C-130 aerial transports. Air cover was supposed to be furnished for the latter part of the operation by a squadron of U.S. fighter planes flying from the *Nimitz*. The actual storming of the embassy and freeing of the prisoners were scheduled to take only about two hours.

Operation Eagle Claw at best was a fanciful, Hollywood-type rescue scenario. The operation broke down in its early stages, which was probably fortunate for the hostages, who might all have been killed by their captors as soon as they were alerted. It was, however, fatally unfortunate for a number of the raiders.

Shortly after the helicopters took off from the *Nimitz* on their 600-mile flight to Desert One, one of the choppers was forced down by rotor blade trouble, and a second chopper returned to the *Nimitz* after its pilot was virtually blinded by a huge dust- or sandstorm. The six remaining helicopters reached their rendezvous point with the transports but one of the six had to be scrapped because of partial hydraulic failure due to the constant blowing of sand in the high desert winds. The possibility of a sandstorm during the operation apparently had not been taken into prior consideration.

When it was reported to President Carter in Washington that there were now only five serviceable helicopters available to proceed to Desert Two, Carter ordered that the mission be aborted. This, however, did not end the fiasco. During refueling for the return flight the sandstorm continued, and three additional helicopters were declared inoperable. One of these damaged choppers accidentally collided with a Hercules transport. Both vehicles burst into flames, killing eight American servicemen. The remaining members of the aborted mission then fled, fearing detection and capture by the Iranian army. They left behind not only their dead but weapons, maps, and a number of secret documents regarding the operation as well as the repairable helicopters.

The last "casualty" was Secretary of State Cyrus Vance. Not learning of the operation he so strongly opposed until it was under way, Vance said he would withhold the announcement of his resignation until the mission was completed. He then lived up to his word, resigned, and was replaced by the former senator from Maine, Edmund Muskie. It was Secretary of State Muskie's unenviable task to try and restore what had once been good relations between Iran and the United States. Muskie's low-key diplomatic approach would finally result in the release of the hostages—but not until January 20, 1981, some 444 days after they were first taken prisoner. Their release date would be the inauguration day for a new United States President, Ronald W. Reagan.

President Reagan and his aides would at first bask in the warm glow of the hostages' return, but soon the Reagan administration would also become entangled in its own peculiar hostage-related affair with Iran. And when Reagan left office and was succeeded in the presidency by George Bush, the hostage problem in the Middle East would still not be solved. Bush, like Carter and Reagan, would be threatened by the continued taking of Americans as hostages, no longer in Iran but in Lebanon, where Iran's influence was powerful enough to inspire continued anti-American actions.

In order to understand how a small Middle East country no larger than Alaska could humiliate a superpower like the United States—and virtually bring down two U.S. presidents and seriously threaten a third—it is necessary for us to learn something of the long history of Iran.

THE RISE AND FALL
OF THE SHAH

One of the oldest countries in the world, Iran—or Persia, as it was called until 1935—had its beginnings some 2,500 years ago. It is situated in southwestern Asia with the Caspian Sea on the north and the Persian Gulf and Gulf of Oman on the south. Its neighbors are the Soviet Union on the north, Turkey and Iraq on the west, Saudi Arabia on the south, and Pakistan and Afghanistan on the east.

Because of its location Persia was a crossroads of early civilization in the Middle East, and for the same reason the country was conquered and occupied from time to time by various peoples—the Greeks, Parthians, Arabs, Turks, and finally the Mongols. Although the Persians and Arabs had different early origins and backgrounds, it was the Arabs who imposed their religious faith on the Persians. This was Islam, the Muslim faith based on the teachings of Mohammed. Eventually Persia was ruled by a series of shahs or kings. Under these shahs the Shia or Shiite sect of the Muslim faith became Persia's state religion.

By the late nineteenth and early twentieth centuries, teachers and missionaries from the United States, Great Britain, France, and other European nations began to introduce new ideas about religious and political freedom into Persia. The missionaries did not have much success teaching Christianity but they did succeed in planting ideas about democracy among the Muslims. In 1906, the Persian people's demands for a constitution and representative government resulted in the nation receiving not only its first constitution but also its first legislative assembly called the Majlis. Up until this time the shahs had ruled as absolute monarchs.

In 1908, oil was discovered in Persia. Competition for control of this "black gold" increased the interest of foreign nations in gaining complete control of the country. Britain, for example, had just converted its entire naval war fleet from the use of coal to oil for fuel and saw the prospect of Persian ports as refueling stations as an ideal arrangement. The industrial nations of Europe as well as the United States also wanted Persia's petroleum for their motor vehicles and factories.

During World War I, Persia once again became a battlefield. Now the oil fields became a top prize. In this latter struggle the British and the Russians became temporary allies to fight against the Germans and Turks. There was also a struggle to control a so-called "Berlin to Baghdad" railway across Persia, which had been partially built by the Germans. By the end of the war no one really controlled the country. Taking advantage of this state of near anarchy, an army colonel by the name of Reza Khan led several thousand of his men into Tehran and set up an emergency government. This was in 1921. By 1925, the Majlis declared that Reza was now the shah and thus established a new dynasty known as Pahlavi. Under Reza Shah Pahlavi much of Great Britain and Russia's mutual grip on the country was eased. Advisers were brought in from the United States to consult on economic and technical problems. Soon the cross-country railway as well as other railways throughout the nation were completed, and

Persia's finances—mainly based, of course, on its large oil output—were on a sound footing.

The first Americans in Persia were missionaries who arrived in the nineteenth century. They established schools in which several thousand students were eventually enrolled. But the Shiite Muslims were not interested in Christianity. Moreover, foreigners, particularly the British and the Russians, were growing in number and strengthening their political inference. The Persian people resented this dominance and resulting interference in their affairs, and came to look kindly on the apparently unselfish Americans. The Americans seemed to have no secret plans to try to control the country but appeared to be satisfied with merely gaining the Persians' respect.

During both this period of development and later, under the guidance of American advisers, Persia made powerful strides in its self-determination as a country. Its legislature agreed that the nation should now be known as Iran as an expression of independence from its immediate past. The name comes from *Ariana*, the word the ancient Greeks and Romans first used to describe the Iranian geographic region. Efforts were also made to develop small manufacturing so that Iran's economy would not be based on a single product—oil.

But as the nation strode forward toward self-sufficiency, Reza Shah Pahlavi became more and more a ruthless dictator. He greatly strengthened the nation's military forces and eliminated elections. Politically the shah found himself in greater sympathy with Germany's dictator, Adolf Hitler, than he was with any Soviet, British, or American leaders. Consequently, American advisers began to be sent home to be replaced by advisers from Germany. Germany, of course, was vitally interested in having Iran as an ally if for nothing more than to fuel its war machine.

After World War II started, Britain, the United States, and the Soviet Union eventually became allies. As allies they were not about to allow their common enemy, Germany, to take over Iran. Not only were they too keenly interested in Iranian oil but Iran was also a direct route to the Soviet Union, to which the United States was soon sending supplies and war matériel. In the late summer of 1941, both the Soviet Union and Britain invaded Iran. The shah's highly touted army fell back in disorder, and the shah himself was driven into exile. When it entered the war in late 1941, the United States also helped to occupy Iran. The exiled shah, who died in South Africa on July 6, 1944, was replaced as the ruler of Iran by his 22-year-old son, Mohammed Reza Pahlavi. He, of course, ruled at the consent of the occupying Allied powers. At their insistence Iran declared war against Germany in September of 1943.

The youthful shah was politically smart enough to realize that after the war his country might simply be divided and taken over by Great Britain and the Soviet Union. Consequently, he began to court the United States, which seemed to favor an independent postwar Iran. Once again American advisers began to flood into the country along with an increase in U.S. military forces. During the war, on Dec. 1, 1943, an important meeting of the Allied leaders—Winston Churchill, Joseph Stalin, and Franklin D. Roosevelt—was held in Tehran to chart the continued course of the conflict. At this meeting Roosevelt spoke out in favor of Iranian postwar independence.

After the war Great Britain and the United States both withdrew their military forces from Iran, but the Soviet Union at first refused to leave the northern provinces. It finally did so but left behind numerous agents who tried to get this area of the country to secede from Iran and join the Soviet Union. Iran finally had to send its own military forces into this area to drive out the Soviets.

During the course of the war an Iranian politician named Mohammed Mossadegh had gradually risen to power. Mossadegh, who became prime minister of Iran on April 30, 1951, headed a nationalist party that wanted to end all foreign interference in Iranian affairs. This meant, among other things, nationalizing the Iranian oil industry and thus eliminating Great Britain's Anglo-Iranian Oil Company, which had been operating in the country since 1909. Mossadegh succeeded in getting his nationalization bill approved by the Majlis and signed by the shah. As a result, Britain was forced to close down its oil field operations and withdraw its oil crews.

From this point forward Mossadegh became more and more dictatorial, and soon he was competing with the shah himself for control of the country. For support the shah leaned more and more heavily on the United States, which was only too happy to strengthen its ties with Iran, by now a key outpost in the Middle East. It was not long, in fact, before many Iranians began complaining about the United States having too much influence in Iranian affairs. The truth of the matter was that not many people really knew just how much the United States was actually supporting the shah. This was because the U.S. Central Intelligence Agency (CIA) was now taking charge of this support, and the CIA's methods were mainly covert or secret. For example, they managed to get several CIA agents into Mossadegh's inner circle of aides, where they learned about all of his future plans.

In the spring of 1953, the CIA made plans to topple Mossadegh from power, claiming the Iranian prime minister was scheming to let the Soviet Union's communists regain much of the old Russian control within Iran. The truth of this claim was doubtful but the shah was such a stout anti-communist that he was willing to believe it. This helped ally him with the CIA's efforts to discredit Mossadegh. The CIA's plan for getting involved in Iran's internal political affairs was called Operation Ajax. In the spring and early summer of 1953, CIA agents hired mobs of Iranians to stir up trouble throughout the country. They also obtained the support of the Iranian military forces, and British intelligence agents secretly aided the operation.

The CIA-sponsored uprising against Mossadegh and his nationalists began in mid-August. At first the uprising seemed to have failed when the man sent by the shah to arrest Mossadegh was captured and executed. But several days later, on August 19, street fighting resumed in Tehran, and Mossadegh was forced to flee. He was arrested in flight, and the shah seemed to have triumphed. Later Mossadegh was sentenced to three years in prison.

But the affair left a bitter taste in the mouths of many Iranians. Hundreds of civilians had been killed in the street fighting, and as word began to leak out about the secret role played by the United States in keeping the shah on his throne there was for the first time a strong current of anti-Americanism abroad in the land. Mossadegh's nationalist cause had been one with which Iranians in general sympathized, and they strongly resented having yet another foreign nation interfere with their country's affairs. To say the least, America's bright image had become badly tarnished.

Meanwhile the shah ignored any misgivings his subjects might have had about American intervention. Instead he seemed more determined than ever to stamp out every last ounce of opposition to his leadership that might remain among his people. He did so primarily by forming in 1957 a powerful secret body of police whose members were instructed to be totally ruthless in seeking out and eliminating government enemies. Called SAVAK (the initials in Persian stood for the "Intelligence and Security Organization of the Country"), this police organization became one of the most feared enforcement agencies in the world. Patterned after intelligence services in both the United States and Israel, SAVAK also adopted the police state torture methods of the KGB in the Soviet Union. In fact as time went on and SAVAK became more and more brutal in its interrogation methods, its Tehran headquarters became as notorious and as feared as the KGB headquarters at 2 Dzerzhinsky Square in Moscow.

The shah further protected his dictatorial reign by signing oil agreements with several European countries as well as the United States. These agreements assured Iran of more than sufficient income to create economic prosperity. The only trouble was that most of this money was used by the shah, his aides, and other wealthy Iranian businessmen before the poor could benefit from any of it. This led to a certain amount of unrest, but the fear of reprisals from SAVAK kept most dissidents silent.

Meanwhile, the shah and the United States continued to expand their friendship. Both military and economic aid were extended to Iran by the administration of President Dwight D. Eisenhower. Between 1953 and 1960, more than $1 billion in such aid was given to Iran, and the shah continued to press for even greater grants. To further cement the Iran-U.S. friendship, Vice-President Richard M. Nixon and his wife Pat visited Iran, and in return the shah and his wife, Queen Soraya, paid an extended visit to the United States. During this visit the Shah met with President Eisenhower on several formal occasions.

The shah's courting of the United States continued into the administration of President John F. Kennedy. The shah and his new wife, Empress Farah, visited the United States, this time paying not only official calls on the president but also traveling extensively throughout the country. The shah even addressed a joint session of the U.S. Congress, emphasizing his nation's close ties with America. In return for the shah's visit, President Kennedy sent his vice-president, Lyndon Johnson, on an official state visit shortly before Kennedy was assassinated in 1963.

When Johnson took over as president he became preoccupied with the Vietnam War in which the United States was then engaged. But Johnson was not so busy that he completely forgot about Iran. American interests in the Persian Gulf area had to be protected, and the shah made it clear Iran would provide this protection. To aid Iran in this role the United States sent a military mission as well as continued military aid. This eventually led to further misunderstanding between many Iranians and the United States.

In 1964, the Iranian legislative assembly passed an extremely controversial law that gave American military personnel serving there the same immunity from Iranian law that all foreign diplomats enjoyed. This meant that American troops and their officers, as well as their families, could not be tried in Iranian courts for any crimes they may have committed in Iran. Because Iranian law was so much different from U.S. military law—much harsher in most cases—the United States had been pushing for just such a law for a long time. But its final passage, by a narrow margin, increased the resentment the average Iranian citizens felt toward all Americans. They felt they were being discriminated against, and that once again a foreign power was in at least partial control of their government.

One of the people who was most outspoken in opposition to this so-called Status of Forces Agreement (SOFA)—it was called "the Capitulation Agreement" by irate Iranians—was the Ayotollah Ruhollah Khomeini.

He lashed out against the agreement, saying it "reduced the Iranian people to a level lower than that of an American dog." Khomeini went on to accuse all those who had promoted SOFA as "traitors." This accusation, of course, included the shah. Because Khomeini was a well-known Muslim religious leader, the shah could not risk having him imprisoned by SAVAK. What he could and did risk was having Khomeini deported from the country and sent into exile in Turkey on November 4, 1964. Khomeini made public his vow to one day even the score not only with the shah but also with the United States.

Apparently indifferent to the threats of Khomeini and his followers, the shah and SAVAK continued to maintain savage control of the country well into the 1970s. With five large prisons filled with political prisoners, the shah ordered several new penitentiaries to be built. Amnesty International, a volunteer human rights organization that investigated worldwide prison conditions, reported in the mid-1970s that the Iranian political process was clearly being dominated by police state methods and that SAVAK systematically practiced torture on its political prisoners. Amnesty International said in its annual report for 1977 that it was particularly concerned about the "arbitrary arrest of suspected political opponents, the use of torture . . . executions, and unofficial deaths" in Iran.[1]

Iranian dissidents lashed out not only at the shah's regime but also at the United States. In the early 1970s, several American military men were assassinated, and in the mid-1970s, three American civilians were killed in Tehran. An unsuccessful kidnap attempt was even made on the U.S. Ambassador to Iran, Douglas MacArthur II. Bomb threats were also made against various American installations, and the offices of the U.S. Information Service and the Peace Corps were actually bombed. SAVAK carried out brutal reprisals against these attacks, but the threat of future acts of terrorism did not diminish.

Human rights, however, did not play a large role on the American political agenda, at least insofar as Iran was concerned. When Richard Nixon became president, he and his National Security Adviser, Henry Kissinger, kept in the shah's good graces both by visiting Iran and increasing the flow of military matériel to that country. Between 1972 and 1977, U.S. arms sales to Iran totaled some $16 billion.

When Jimmy Carter became president in 1977, the shah made some effort to install a more liberal government in Iran. He did this partly because of increasing unrest among his people, especially among the Shiite Muslims. In addition, the shah had been told by his doctors that he was suffering from possibly incurable cancer. This diagnosis made the shah more concerned than ever about the future of the Pahlavi reign. The heir apparent was the shah's teenage son, Crown Prince Reza. But to rule effectively this young man would need the full support of the Iranian people, not merely their forced acceptance of yet one more dictatorial head of a police state.

The shah's half-hearted attempts at political reform included holding elections more often and giving more underprivileged people government jobs. But such reform efforts were a little late in coming. By that time the religious opposition to his oppressive reign gave every indication of developing into a revolution. Carter and his administration gave full support to the shah, but massive Muslim religious demonstrations made it clear that American support would probably not be enough to keep the Pahlavi regime in power. During 1978 and into early 1979, riots against the shah's regime took place in several major Iranian cities. In the riots some 12,000 people were killed and at least 50,000 injured. The distant leader of this revolutionary prelude was the Ayatollah Khomeini, who had been exiled by the shah and was now living in Paris, France.

The man who was to become the Ayatollah Ruhollah Khomeini had been born near Tehran in 1900. Both his mother and father died while Ruhollah was still in his teens, and the youth had been raised by relatives. Interested in the Muslim religion from an early age, Ruhollah studied under several of Iran's best teachers. He himself went on to become a teacher and lecturer in Shiite Muslim philosophy. A part of this philosophy taught that a true Muslim should be willing to give up his life for his religious beliefs. In fact if one did give up his or her life for Allah, one became a true Muslim martyr and would live happily in the hereafter. Death in battle against Islam's enemies became an especially glorious way to attain martyrdom. So firmly was this belief held that in Iran's war against Iraq, which was soon to begin, teenage boys—and some not yet in their teens—readily advanced into the face of murderous enemy fire, sacrificing themselves for Allah. In his teacher's role Khomeini spoke to thousands of youths in the 1930s and 1940s. Gradually he became opposed to the Pahlavi regime and developed into not only a religious leader but also a political activist. Soon he gained the reputation of being a fearless political foe of the shah, which resulted in his exile.

Exile did not silence Khomeini. He issued proclamations calling for the downfall of the Pahlavi government and demanding a revolution by the poor and oppressed Iranians. These proclamations were distributed throughout Iran and soon the exiled ayatollah became a legendary folk hero to his people. In attacking the shah, the ayatollah always simultaneously attacked the United States for its support of the Iranian police state. This caused increasing alarm in the United States, which considered the shah a pillar of strength in the Middle East. While he was running for the presidency, Jimmy Carter had made several speeches condemning American support of Iran and that country's poor record regarding human rights. Yet, after he was elected president, Carter and his administration followed in the footsteps of earlier U.S. administrations and leaned heavily on the Pahlavi pillar. Consequently, Carter and his State Department spoke out strongly in support of the shah and in opposition to the religious revolutionary leader Khomeini.

But now the shah himself began to waiver in the face of the fierce opposition to his reign. He had no real desire to have his country drown in a bloodbath of civil war that might well follow the revolutionary unrest. In addition, the knowledge of his own mortal illness undoubtedly robbed the shah of much of his former stubborn determination to rule Iran with an iron hand. For whatever reason or combination of reasons, the shah surprised the Western world in general—and the United States in particular—when he and his wife and family and a small group of aides suddenly boarded the royal Iranian Boeing 707 aircraft on January 16, 1979, and flew out of the country, never to return.

Once the shah fled the country, the Iranian revolution became a full-blown affair. In the midst of the revolutionary chaos the Ayatollah Khomeini returned and was soon the nation's new leader. Meanwhile, the self-exiled shah found he was truly a man without a country. Because of his close ties with the United States it was at first thought he would seek refuge in America. But spokespersons for President Carter made it clear that the United States would not welcome the shah. It was obvious that fear of Iranian retaliation prompted this decision. Consequently, for many months the exiled shah and his family had to find temporary homes in Egypt, Morocco, the Bahamas, Panama, and Mexico.

The shah, however, still had champions in the United States. Among them were former National Security Adviser and Secretary of State Henry Kissinger, banker David Rockefeller, and diplomat John J. McCloy. These three men rallied other influential political leaders to persuade President Carter to allow the shah to enter the country—for humanitarian reasons—to be treated for his cancer. The shah survived gall bladder surgery on October 26, 1979. A little more than a week later, on November 4, the Iranians retaliated by taking over the American embassy in Tehran and holding its occupants hostage. While the hostage siege was going on in Tehran, the shah left the United States and eventually returned to Egypt. There on July 27, 1980, he died of a massive internal hemorrhage in a Cairo hospital. But his death did not end the Iranian militants' demands for the fortune the shah had taken with him, and for the Iranian deposits frozen in American banks. In its dealings with the Iranian militants the United States continued to freeze these funds as a lever to try and pry the hostages loose.

Although the shah died in the summer of 1980, it was not until January 19, 1981, that Khomeini agreed to the release of the hostages. He did so mainly because the United States was about to inaugurate a new president, Ronald Reagan, and Iranian leaders wanted Reagan to lift the U.S. economic sanctions against their country as well as to return $12 billion in Iranian assets frozen in U.S. banks. Iran was now fighting a war with its neighbor, Iraq, and badly needed all the funds it could get.

In return for the hostages, the United States agreed to refrain from interfering in Iran's private affairs, to settle private American claims against Iran, to freeze all of the shah's assets until Iran presented its due claims, and to transfer all Iranian assets in U.S. banks to accounts controlled by an intermediary country—Algeria. On January

20, 1981, shortly after his inauguration, President Reagan announced to the world that two planes carrying the fifty-two American hostages had left Iran. Thus ended the 444-day siege that had begun in November of 1979.

President Reagan could well afford to be generous about the hostages. They had been a major reason for his defeat of Jimmy Carter in the 1980 presidential election. To express his magnanimity Reagan sent Carter as the official U.S. emissary to greet the hostages when they arrived in Wiesbaden, West Germany, the first stop on their return journey home. There they were examined at the U.S. Air Force Hospital following their formal release, and all were in reasonably good health.

Upon their actual return to the United States a few days later, the hostages were greeted as heroes by President Reagan who said, "Let terrorists be aware that when the rules of international behavior are violated, our policy will be one of swift and effective retribution. . . . There are limits to our patience."[2]

The president would soon have ample opportunity to try to live up to his words, for during the next decade numerous other Americans were taken hostage in the Middle East. Hostage-taking, in fact, seemed to have become standard operating procedure by Shiite Muslim terrorists sponsored by Iran.

PRESIDENT REAGAN FACES A NEW HOSTAGE CRISIS

While the fifty-two hostages were being held in Iran, many Americans sang a popular song of the day, "Tie a Yellow Ribbon Round the Old Oak Tree." They also publicly displayed yellow ribbons, flags, and other decorations to show their faithful belief in the eventual return of the hostages. Once the hostages were freed, the yellow decorations were quickly taken down and the public seemed eager to put the hostage crisis out of their minds.

The United States government also seemed eager to forget about the past and go about its business of running the country under a new administration. Ronald Reagan became one of the most popular presidents in American history. This popularity continued almost to the end of his first term in office. Then the ugly word "hostage" once again was seen and heard daily in the press and on television.

When the grim business of hostage-taking began again it was not in Iran but in another Middle East country, Lebanon. But there was an Iranian connection. The hostages were being taken by various branches of an organization known as the Hezbollah, or Party of God. The Party of God had been founded in Iran and exported to Lebanon, where its leaders still took their orders from the Ayatollah Khomeini and other militant Iranian Muslims.

It was never clear what, if anything, in particular prompted the new wave of hostage-taking. A part of it was no doubt due to Khomeini's sheer hatred of the United States. Part was also due to the fact that not all of Iran's assets frozen in the United States had yet been returned to Iran because various claims still had to be settled in the courts. And part was involved in the ongoing warfare between Palestinians and Israel over whether or not the Palestinians should be allowed to establish their homeland in Lebanon. From time to time the Israelis captured and held prisoner various Palestinians. To get these prisoners released the Palestinians accepted Khomeini's suggestion that hostages be taken with the intention that these hostages could be traded for the imprisoned Palestinians. Since the United States was a close ally of Israel, taking Americans as hostages might make the United States put pressure on Israel to release the prisoners.

But the United States announced loudly and clearly to the world that it would make no deals for hostages. Experts agreed that this was the only way to handle the matter; if a country began to make hostage deals, the hostage-taking would go on indefinitely, with new hostages being taken as soon as others were released. The United States not only announced its "no deals for hostages" position but it also persuaded its allies—Great Britain and France in particular—to make similar announcements. This was important because British and French citizens were also being taken hostage in Lebanon.

The renewed kidnapping of American hostages began early in 1984. On February 10 of that year Frank Reiger, a professor of electrical engineering at the American University in Beirut, was seized. Reiger, however, managed to escape two months later, on April 15.

On March 7, 1984, Jeremy Levin, the Mid-East Bureau Chief for television's Cable News Network, was captured. He too eventually escaped but not until the following year, on February 14, 1985.

On March 16, 1984, William Buckley was captured. Buckley's kidnapping caused quite a stir, especially behind locked doors in Washington, because he was the Central Intelligence Agency's station chief in Beirut, and it was feared he would be tortured to get him to reveal the names of other CIA agents in the Middle East.

Two other Americans captured in Lebanon in 1984 were Rev. Benjamin Weir, a Presbyterian minister, kidnapped on May 8; and Peter Kilburn, a librarian at Beirut's American University, kidnapped December 3. Kilburn's dead body was found on April 17, 1986.

While there was a certain amount of public outcry in the United States when each of these persons was taken hostage, it in no way matched the nationwide concern expressed during the Iran embassy hostage crisis. Many people did, however, ask why the United States didn't do something about the situation. The truth of the matter was there was very little of an open-and-aboveboard nature that the United States could do. For one thing no one seemed to know just where the hostages were being held, so an Entebbe-like raid was out of the question. Secondly, military action against Iran or the Palestinians in Lebanon might send the whole Middle East up in flames in a general war.

While the new outbreak of hostage-taking did not exactly add to President Reagan's popularity, amazingly it seemed to do very little to harm it. When the time came for his reelection to a second term, Reagan had no trouble being renominated and then reelected in the fall of 1984. He easily defeated the Democratic presidential nominee, Walter Mondale.

Unfortunately, the taking of American hostages in the Middle East continued well into President Reagan's second term. On January 8, 1985, a few days before Reagan was again sworn into office, the Rev. Lawrence Martin Jenco, a Roman Catholic priest, was captured and held prisoner somewhere in Lebanon.

On May 16, 1985, Terry A. Anderson, chief Middle East correspondent for the Associated Press, was also seized. On May 28, 1985, David P. Jacobsen, director of the American University of Beirut hospital, was kidnapped. And on June 9, 1985, the acting Dean of Agriculture at the American University, Thomas Sutherland, was also captured. (In 1986 three more hostages would be taken, in 1987 four more, and another in 1988. This did not include Americans taken hostage elsewhere in various airplane hijackings and other acts of terrorism.)

As public criticism once again began to mount over the Reagan administration's lack of response to these kidnappings, the Presbyterian minister, Rev. Benjamin F. Weir, was suddenly released on September 15, 1985. A few months later, on July 26, 1986, the Roman Catholic priest, Father Lawrence M. Jenco, was also set free. No public explanation was given for the release of these men, but the media speculated that the fact that they were religious leaders may have been a factor. No further questions were asked until November 2, 1986, when hospital administrator David P. Jacobsen was released. Immediately a story broke in a Middle East publication that caught the attention of the American press.

The story involving Jacobsen appeared in the November 3 edition of a weekly Lebanese newspaper called *Al-Shiraa*. In it, editor Hassan Sabra reported that Robert McFarlane, a former top aide of President Reagan's, had just completed a secret but official visit to Tehran, Iran, where he had tried to arrange an arms-for-hostages deal between the United States and the Khomeini regime.

The American press were at first inclined to ignore

the *Al-Shiraa* story as just another propaganda piece, but they did note the fact that the story appeared on the same weekend that hostage Jacobsen was flown out of Beirut, Lebanon, to Cyprus and then to the United States. White House reporters asked presidential press secretary Larry Speakes about McFarlane's reported trip to Tehran. Speakes promptly denied any knowledge of such a trip.

When McFarlane was asked how much truth there was to the story, he said it was all "a piece of pure fiction."[1] The U.S. State Department also supported Speakes and McFarlane.

But on November 6, two U.S. newspapers, the *Washington Post* and the *Los Angeles Times*, carried front-page stories declaring that for some months secret arms-for-hostages talks had been taking place between the United States and Iran.

Both of these newspapers had played important investigative roles in what was known as the Watergate Affair back in the early 1970s. This notorious affair had eventually caused Richard M. Nixon to become the first American president to resign from office. Republican Nixon had lied about trying to cover up a burglary attempt at the Democratic party national headquarters in the Watergate apartment and office complex in Washington, D.C. The purpose of the burglary was to steal the opposition's election campaign plans and to install electronic "bugs" or eavesdropping devices to gain access to key conversations among the opposition party's leaders. Because both newspapers had been so accurate in reporting the Watergate Affair, the American public was more than willing to believe they were telling the truth now about secret U.S. dealings with Iran.

The revelation was, of course, shocking to most people. In their minds were still vivid pictures of the Americans being held hostage at the U.S. embassy in Tehran. Khomeini and his people were still the enemy. Americans recalled only too well seeing their country insulted by the Tehran militants burning American flags and hanging dummy figures of President Carter and other U.S. leaders. Could America's own much-loved President Reagan have forgotten so quickly? If not, what possessed him to be making shady deals with the despised Iranian leaders?

The president at first flatly denied that either he or his vice president, George Bush, had known anything about any arms-for-hostages deals. But his critics would not accept his denials. Back during the Watergate Affair, Senator Howard Baker had been among those who thought that President Nixon had known about the Watergate burglary even though he denied such knowledge. Baker had taken to asking the question repeatedly, "What did President Nixon know, and when did he know it?" Now that question was resurrected and rephrased to enquire, "What did President Reagan know, and when did he know it?"

Finally the public clamor reached such a crescendo that some sort of public statement by the president seemed necessary. On November 13, 1986, President Reagan went on television from the White House and declared:

> The charge has been made that the United States has shipped weapons to Iran as ransom payment for the release of American hostages in Lebanon; that the United States undercut its allies and secretly violated American policy against trafficking with terrorists.
>
> Those charges are utterly false. The United States has not made concessions to those who hold our people captive in Lebanon. And we will not. The United States has not swapped boatloads

or planeloads of American weapons for the return of American hostages. And we will not.[2]

Contradicting the president's statement was the fact—not revealed until later—that as far back as December 1985 the Reagan administration had persuaded Dale Van Atta, a partner of newspaper columnist Jack Anderson, not to break the story of the arms-for-hostages deal with Iran. Van Atta had written such an article and submitted it to the White House to see if it violated national security.

And Barbara Honegger, presidential aide and member of the Department of Justice during the Reagan era, also later declared that there had been an arms-for-hostages deal with Iran even before the current one. In her book, *October Surprise*, Honegger wrote that when Reagan was running against Jimmy Carter for the presidency in 1980, the Reaganites' greatest fear was of "an eleventh-hour release of the U.S. hostages (that is, before the Reagan-Carter election) which they knew could sweep President Carter to an almost certain victory."[3] Consequently, Honegger claimed, the Reagan campaign negotiated a $40 million sale of weapons to sabotage President Carter's attempts to free the hostages and thus defeat his re-election effort. The release of the fifty-two hostages was then arranged to take place only after Reagan actually became president. The 1986 arms-for-hostages deal, according to Honegger, was simply an extension of the 1980 deal.[4]

Reagan himself as much as admitted the truth of the arms-for-hostages deal a short time after his initial denial, only this time he qualified the admission by claiming a third country, Israel, had been involved. Shortly after making that statement he once again denied it. Finally, he said, "I don't remember—period."[5]

Eventually, on March 4, 1987, Reagan said: "What

began as a strategic opening to Iran deteriorated into trading arms for hostages."[6]

The American public continued to be highly critical of such questionable activities by their government. Reagan's popularity fell to an all-time low, and it was many months before it rose to anywhere near its previous level. Meanwhile, the hostage problem remained unsolved.

ARMS-FOR-HOSTAGES

The United States arms-for-hostages deals with Iran actually began in 1985. The deals were arranged through Robert McFarlane, who was then National Security Adviser and head of the National Security Council (NSC).

The NSC had been formed in 1947 shortly after the end of World War II. At this time a so-called Cold War had developed between the Soviet Union and the United States, and American government officials believed it was important to have secret information about the military plans of the Russians. The Central Intelligence Agency, which was also established in 1947, and U.S. military intelligence agencies were supposed to gather this information, all of which would be given to the NSC. The NSC in turn, through the National Security Adviser, would then give the president and other key members of the government the important parts of this secret information or intelligence. Members of the NSC besides the National Security Adviser are by law the president, vice president, secretary of state, secretary of defense, and anyone else the president chooses.

One of NSC Adviser McFarlane's staff members was a young Marine lieutenant colonel named Oliver North. Colonel North had been engaged in secret activities for the government for many months. Some of these activities McFarlane knew about but others he did not. During the course of his secret or clandestine work Colonel North learned that Israel was selling arms to Iran for use in its war with Iraq. When North reported these arms sales to his boss, McFarlane promptly reported them to President Reagan. As a result, an official complaint was made to Israel by the U.S. government. But this complaint was ignored on the grounds that Israel needed the money from these arms sales to support its own struggling economy. Eventually it was out of this Israeli business arrangement with Iran that the U.S. arms-for-hostages deals with Iran began.

Among the many questionable characters Colonel North had gotten acquainted with in his secret activities was an ex-Iranian official named Manucher Ghorbanifar. Ghorbanifar was said to be a former member of the shah's secret police, SAVAK. He had fled from Iran in 1980. In exile he had tried to make connections with the CIA, but the CIA put little faith in him. For one thing he had failed to pass lie detector tests regarding his background. But at first Colonel North and later McFarlane stoutly supported Ghorbanifar, who told them he had deliberately flunked the lie detector tests because he didn't really want to work for the CIA.

It was apparently Ghorbanifar who first suggested that the United States could cover its tracks in an arms-for-hostages deal with Iran by using Israel as a third party or broker in the scheme. Ghorbanifar suggested the plan to David Kimche, an Israeli diplomat experienced in covert or secret operations. In a meeting with McFarlane in his White House office on July 3, 1985, Kimche passed along Ghorbanifar's plan. It was simple enough. The United States would sell whatever war matériel that was needed by Iran to Israel, and Israel would in turn deliver the goods to

Iran. In exchange the United States would not only gain the money from the arms sales but Ghorbanifar also guaranteed that Iran would see to it that the American hostages held in Lebanon would be released.

McFarlane delivered this proposal to President Reagan who, according to McFarlane's later testimony, was enthusiastic about it. He was especially excited about the possibility of the release of the hostages. But McFarlane was temporarily kept from further action when Reagan was hospitalized through the rest of the month for an intestinal cancer operation.

Nevertheless, while Reagan was still in the hospital recuperating, McFarlane again talked with him about the arms sale, and the president continued to approve of it. Still no action was taken.

When the president returned to the White House he called a meeting to discuss the arms sale. In addition to Reagan and McFarlane those present at the August 6 meeting were reported to be Secretary of State George Shultz, Secretary of Defense Caspar Weinberger, and Vice President George Bush. Bush later insisted he did not attend this meeting, but the others present claimed he did.

This was the first time that Shultz and Weinberger had heard about the proposed deal, and they were flatly against it. Both men were still smarting from Khomeini's seizure of the hostages at the American embassy in Tehran and his insulting remarks about "the Great Satan" that continued even after the hostages were released. They were also sure that the majority of the American people felt exactly the same way they did about Khomeini and Iran. McFarlane tried to point out that the Iranians the U.S. would be dealing with through Israel were Iranian moderates, not fanatical followers of Khomeini. Further, the release of the American hostages in Lebanon would soothe the American public's ruffled feelings about its government making deals with Iran.

The meeting ended with no decision having been clearly made, but according to Bob Schieffer and Gary Paul Gates in their book, *The Acting President*, "Each of the participants was inclined to interpret the President's passivity as a subtle sign of concurrence."[1] What they meant was that Reagan had said very little during the discussion and each of the participants thought the president's silence meant he was agreeing with their viewpoint. Also, according to Schieffer and Gates, plus McFarlane's own later testimony, "A day or so after the August 6 meeting, Reagan telephoned him [McFarlane], and gave him unequivocal approval to tell the Israelis that he had authorized the plan."[2]

But Reagan himself later insisted he could not recall having made any such telephone call to McFarlane. Whatever the truth or lack of it in these statements, McFarlane instructed North to go ahead and work out the deal with Ghorbanifar and the Israelis.

The first shipment of U.S.-made arms in this three-way deal went from Israel to Iran early in September. This shipment consisted of 500 anti-tank missiles. In mid-September a second shipment went forward.

At this point Kimche told McFarlane that just one hostage would now be released. This was Rev. Benjamin Weir. Ghorbanifar assured North, however, that continued arms shipments would result in the release of additional hostages. But this time the weapons desired were more sophisticated. Iraq was making almost daily air raids on Iran with high level bombers. What the Iranians wanted—via Israel, of course—were anti-aircraft missiles that were capable of shooting down these bombers.

Again McFarlane turned over the handling of the details of the deal to Oliver North and told him flatly not to ship any weapons until the hostages had actually been released. But North was so eager to keep the deal going that he allowed Israel to ship the arms before any hostages were set free. This time the deal backfired when an angry Ghorbanifar told North that all of the anti-aircraft missiles were old and out of date and incapable of hitting high-altitude bombers. North promised to do better next time.

There was a curious aftermath to this episode. On December 12, 1985, a chartered DC-8 transport plane carrying 256 people crashed while taking off after a refueling stop at Gander, Newfoundland. All aboard were killed. The dead passengers were members of the U.S. 101st Airborne Division returning from duty in the Middle East. Immediately after the crash it was believed that icing on the plane's wings caused the fatal accident. But veteran flyers disagreed. There were also eyewitnesses who said there had been an explosion aboard the plane before it crashed. There then was speculation about the contents of several mysterious crates that had been put aboard the plane at an earlier stop in Cairo, Egypt. Could these crates have contained explosives with timing devices? Out of this speculation grew the theory that the United States was simply being repaid for the useless anti-aircraft missiles it had sold Iran in late November. Nothing has ever been proved or disproved about this story, nor has the cause of the plane crash definitely been determined, although it's been reported that the DC-8 had had a history of mechanical problems.

McFarlane was furious with North for letting the second deal go through with no positive results so far as the United States was concerned. McFarlane was also having difficulty getting along with President Reagan's chief of staff, Donald Regan, who constantly tried to keep McFarlane from personally seeing and conferring with the president. McFarlane was not the only presidential aide with whom Regan dealt in this high-handed manner. Regan was the kind of chief of staff who thought that all contacts with the president should be funneled through him and made matters difficult for those who tried to go around him. This was typical of the difficult kind of bureaucratic infighting in which McFarlane had been engaged for several years, and he had grown sick and tired of it. What he probably needed was a long vacation or at least a temporary change of scene. To achieve just that he abruptly decided to resign as National Security Adviser.

McFarlane, it was later reported, thought that President Reagan would try to talk him out of resigning. But Reagan simply thanked him for his loyal service and promptly named Rear Admiral John M. Poindexter, a Navy man experienced in administration, to take over as National Security Adviser. Several of Reagan's aides did not think a military man should serve in this post; they also thought Poindexter had other shortcomings, such as inexperience in diplomacy. Nevertheless, the appointment went through.

As soon as Poindexter took over as McFarlane's replacement North proposed yet one more arms-for-hostages deal with Iran. By this time North had a powerful additional reason for keeping these deals going: he had realized that a considerable amount of money could be made from selling the arms to Iran and that this money could be used for North's other secret project (to be discussed in Chapter 5).

When Poindexter told North to go ahead with the new arms-for-hostages deal, North made plans to fly to London to confer with Ghorbanifar. By now both North and Ghorbanifar had just about decided to omit using Israel as a middleman and to deal directly with the Iranians. This method, the shrewd Ghorbanifar insisted, would be much more effective with the "moderate" Iranians since no Iranians liked working with the Israelis because of their religious differences. He did not point out that the Iranians up to now also had differences, both religious and secular, with the "Great Satan" United States.

President Reagan made a point of calling at least one more top level meeting of his aides to discuss the sale of arms to Iran in exchange for hostages. Included among those present at this meeting early in January 1986 were Shultz, Weinberger, Poindexter, Regan, and the president, plus CIA Director William Casey, Attorney General Edwin Meese, and Vice President George Bush. At this meeting the president clearly favored the continuation of the Iran operation. Shultz and Weinberger continued to bluntly oppose it. Poindexter, Casey, Meese, and Bush all indicated their approval, but Bush later claimed it had never been quite clear to him that what they were talking about was actually an arms-for-hostages deal. What he *did* think they were talking about was never clear either.

In his meeting with Ghorbanifar in London, North made plans to sell Iran 1,000 more missiles, this time up-to-date ones called HAWKS. In their book Schieffer and Gates point out exactly how much money North made for his secret project fund from just this one deal in February 1986. Multiply this by perhaps another dozen such deals and it is obvious that this was indeed a financially worthwhile arrangement. "The Iranians paid $10 million for the weapons, and after deducting $4 million for the cost of the transaction, that left $6 million to add to the swelling bankroll."[3]

The only problem was that again no hostages were released.

Because Ghorbanifar had produced no hostages, Poindexter and North decided that he was no longer a reliable go-between. The best way to get the job done, they agreed, was for North himself to go to Iran and there deal directly with the so-called moderates whom Ghorbanifar had been bragging about. But North needed some strong diplomatic support to undertake such a mission. This support was provided by calling upon retired National Security Adviser McFarlane. Reluctantly McFarlane agreed to lead the mission to Tehran.

Of all the foreign operations in which American diplomats have been involved, this one was probably the most ill advised, if not outright foolhardy. Up to this point the attempts to deal with Iran through Ghorbanifar's contacts had produced almost no results as far as obtaining the release of hostages was concerned. Secondly, there was no real proof that there actually existed in Iran moderates who disagreed with the fanatical Khomeini. And finally the United States would be sending into Iran, a country with which it was virtually at war, two men, McFarlane and North, who probably knew as much about top secret U.S. military and foreign policy matters as any two men in American government.

What if the Iranians should simply seize McFarlane and North and force them through torture to disclose top secret information? Or McFarlane and North could simply be seized and held as hostages themselves. In hindsight, most observers agreed, it was nothing short of incredible that President Reagan allowed the mission to take place.

North did continue to work with Ghorbanifar in setting up the arrangements for the mission. It was decided that there would be two unmarked Israeli airplanes involved. Both would fly from Tel Aviv to Tehran. One would carry those in the American party who were to participate in the meeting. Also on this plane would be a number of missiles and missile parts. A second plane filled with additional war matériel would remain behind at Tel Aviv and not take off until the hostages had been released.

The first plane left Tel Aviv on May 25, 1986, a hot Sunday morning. It landed at Tehran's Mehrabad International Airport a few hours later. There were no Iranian officials there to greet the Americans and their aides. A band of revolutionaries, however, did surround the plane waving rifles and other weapons threateningly. Finally, after an hour's uneasy wait Iran's Deputy Prime Minister, Abbas Kangarloo, arrived in a jeep. He escorted the Americans to what had been the Royal Hilton Hotel.

After their greeting, or lack of it, at the airport and the long delay there, McFarlane was convinced that their mission was a failure. Further, he even began to fear for his and North's safety. Although they both carried false passports McFarlane was certain that the few Iranians with whom he did manage to talk knew very well who he and North were. He and North were also carrying poison pills with which to commit suicide in case they were taken prisoner, but it wasn't until the talks actually got under way that McFarlane thought they might have to use them.

Kangarloo started off by saying there simply must have been some sort of misunderstanding if the Americans thought any hostages would be exchanged as a result of this particular meeting. The actual purpose of the meeting, Kangarloo said, was to make arrangements for a truly top level meeting between Iranian and American diplomats. Not noted for his ability to control his temper, McFarlane angrily expressed his displeasure over this information.

In response to McFarlane's outburst, the Iranians sent a more senior diplomat to the scene. This man, Hadi Najaf-Abadi, was chairman of Iran's foreign relations committee. Najaf-Abadi won his way into North's if not McFarlane's heart by suggesting the need for the largest multimillion dollar arms deal to date. North immediately saw this as a boon for his secret fund. But McFarlane, who up to this time knew nothing about North's secret fund, kept the issue of the hostages at the forefront of the conversation. When no headway was made on this matter, McFarlane abruptly announced an end to the meeting. McFarlane's firm stand resulted in the announcement by the Iranians on May 28 that Khomeini had agreed to the release of two hostages in Lebanon. These were Father Lawrence Jenco and David Jacobsen. But they were not immediately released.

Despite this offer the angry and disappointed McFarlane continued his preparations to return home. North, however, lingered for a few hours to try to work out some future arms deal. To cement such a deal North saw to it that the second plane bearing missiles took off from Tel Aviv and landed in Tehran before he and McFarlane left. On the way home North told McFarlane for the first time how he was using the surplus funds from the arms sales that he had been secretly gathering. McFarlane was literally speechless at this news, and North took his silence for approval. It was McFarlane, after all, North told himself, who had actually got him started on the deal.

It is not known whether McFarlane told President Reagan about North's secret use of the arms funds when they returned from Iran. North assumed he did, but the president later denied any such knowledge. McFarlane did report to the president that their Iran trip had been a total failure, and for a time Reagan considered taking some sort of military action to rescue the hostages. He talked over such plans with North but nothing actually ever came of them. No one could figure out just how to keep the hostages from being murdered the moment their captors got word such a rescue mission was under way.

Within a relatively short time the Iranians did begin to live up to their promise to release some of the hostages, and White House aides began to wonder if perhaps McFarlane had been too hasty in his angry departure from Tehran. It was pointed out to him that in dealing with so-called "rug merchants" like the Iranians, no deal began until the prospective customer was walking out the door. On July 26 Father Jenco was released. On November 2 David Jacobsen was released, and there was some indication that Terry Anderson would be given his freedom a short time later. The Anderson prediction was not fulfilled.

But just to keep the international hostage crisis at fever pitch, two more American hostages were kidnapped in Lebanon in September 1986 and another in October. These were Frank Herbert Reed, director of the private Lebanon International School in Beirut, kidnapped on September 9; Joseph James Cicippio, acting comptroller of the American University of Beirut, September 12; and Edward Austin Tracy, an author of children's books, October 21.

As has been indicated earlier, no word leaked out to the public about the secret arms-for-hostages deals or about the McFarlane-North trip to Tehran until the late fall of 1986. When the story first began appearing in the press and on television, it dealt strictly with the arms-for-hostages deals. This to most Americans was bad enough, but then a second element surfaced—Colonel North's secret use of funds from the arms sales—and the public began to demand some sort of explanation from the Reagan administration.

And just what was Oliver North's secret fund being used for? The answer was slow in coming and its details emerged piece by piece over the next several months.

OLIVER NORTH AND THE
IRAN-CONTRA AFFAIR

Oliver North's secret fund was used to support an anti-communist organization in Central America that was favored by President Ronald Reagan and his administration. This organization, which was active in Nicaragua, was known as the Contras. In order to understand how and why the United States became so deeply involved with the Contras, it is important to know how and why Reagan became such a strong anti-communist.

Before Reagan became active in state and national politics he had begun an acting career in 1937. As a member of the motion picture industry Reagan was a member of the Screen Actors' Guild, the actors' union organization. Eventually he became the Guild president. At that time he was a liberal Democrat who strongly supported President Franklin Delano Roosevelt's New Deal program, which gave federal aid to programs for the jobless. But the more active he became in the Screen Actors' Guild the more Reagan thought it was being taken over by communists. He also came to believe that the communists were trying to gain control of state and national government in the United States with the purpose of eventually destroying it. Gradually Reagan shifted from left-wing liberalism to right-wing conservatism and his goals became centered on driving the communists out of American life wherever they tried to gain control.

When he became president of the United States, Reagan was convinced that the communists, directly backed by the Soviet Union, were trying to gain control of Central America in general and the country of Nicaragua in particular. From there they would be a direct threat to the United States. One of the aims of the Reagan administration was to drive the communists out of Central America. In Nicaragua, Reagan and his aides opposed the leftist government in power, known as the Sandinistas, and supported a rebel conservative organization known as the Contras. Reagan insisted that the United States was not trying to overthrow the Sandinista government, but this in effect was what it was trying to do.

The Sandinistas and much of the rest of Central America strongly objected to American interference in their political affairs. Since the turn of the twentieth century the United States had interfered in Central America literally dozens of times. In the early 1900s, U.S. Marines had been sent in to Nicaragua to control rebel uprisings. In the late 1920s, the Marines had again returned to "preserve order," and this kind of American intrusion into Central America had become something of a habit. Consequently, not only the citizens of Central America but also many U.S. citizens had objected to the Reagan administration's once again becoming involved in Central American politics.

In addition, the United States had fought and lost a war against another communist government in Vietnam during the 1960s and 1970s. More than 50,000 American youths had died in this war and billions of dollars had been spent in waging it. To many Americans this vast outpouring of blood and resources amounted to sheer waste and they did not want it repeated in Central America. As a result of the Reagan administration's support of the Contras against the Sandinistas in Nicaragua and the public's general lack of support, the U.S. Congress blew hot and cold in supplying funds for the rebel Contra cause.

At first the Congress furnished the funds Reagan asked for to support the Contras. But when there were no immediate results apparent in the fighting between the Contras and the Sandinistas, Congress cut off these funds. In fact, in 1983, Congressman Edward P. Boland of Massachusetts presented a bill forbidding the giving of military aid to the Contras. This bill was passed. It did, however, allow so-called "humanitarian aid," such as food and medical supplies, to be sent.

At this point the Reagan administration began using other methods, all of them highly questionable from an ethical standpoint if not from a legal one, to continue to obtain funds to support the Contras. Wealthy private citizens and even foreign nations were quietly approached and asked to give this aid. The favors promised in return have never been made clear. But the most successful device— successful in terms of funds provided, but legally and constitutionally questionable—was developed by Oliver North. According to the Constitution, only the U.S. Congress is authorized to provide such funds. North's method was simply to secretly use the funds obtained from the sale of arms to Iran for obtaining military matériel and supplies for the Contras. This money probably should have gone into the U.S. Treasury but instead it was used for Reagan's pet anti-communist project. In addition, two of North's partners in the arms deals apparently made a personal profit from them. Eventually the secret use of the arms sale funds by North's self-established government-within-a-government blossomed into the Iran-Contra affair.

It has never been wholly clear just who suggested this

idea to North, but he always claimed that Ghorbanifar did. When this tricky use of these federal funds was suggested, North later admitted he thought it was a "neat idea." North promptly labeled his operation "Project Democracy."[1]

Oliver North was certainly the most colorful of all of the people involved in the Iran hostage crises and the Iran-Contra affair. Few Americans had mixed feelings about him. To some he was a hero. To others he was a loose cannon on board the U.S. ship of state who threatened to destroy it by breaking the law and circumventing the U.S. Constitution. To try to understand him it is important to learn about his early background before he became the central figure in a scandal that for a time threatened the Reagan administration.

To Manucher Ghorbanifar, the Iranian contact man, North was always somewhat unbelievable if not unreal. He described North as an overzealous patriot, who would snap to attention at the sight of any American sign or symbol, such as the American flag or a lighted Coca-Cola sign. There were others who thought North was a sincere superpatriot and always had been. Apparently President Reagan was a member of this school.

Now in his early forties, Lt. Col. Oliver Laurance (Ollie) North was a native of Philmont, a small town in upstate New York where his family had been in the textile business for several generations. He was born, however, at Fort Sam Houston in San Antonio, Texas, on October 7, 1943, while his father, Clay, was on duty there accompanied by his wife, Ann, during World War II. Clay went on to serve with General George Patton's famed Third Army in Europe. He was awarded both the Silver Star and Bronze Star for heroism. When he returned home at war's end, Clay led a Victory Day parade down Philmont's main street while his wife and two-year-old son Ollie looked on.

Ollie led an uneventful life as a boy, although he and his demanding father had difficulty from time to time. The elder North continued to be a dedicated patriot, marching in full uniform in all of the local parades and displaying the American flag on every possible occasion. This attitude, plus his strict disciplinary demands, definitely rubbed off not only on Ollie but also on the other three North children—Patricia, John, and Timothy. Ollie, in fact, was to spend much of his early life trying to live up to standards set by his father.

Interestingly, however, when the time came to choose a career Ollie at first chose to follow in his mother's footsteps and become a teacher. With this end in mind, after graduating from the local high school Ollie enrolled in Brockport State College near Rochester, New York. He attended classes there for two years, but in the summer between his freshman and sophomore years he enlisted in the Marine Corps officer's training program at Camp Lejeune, North Carolina.

Ollie loved the Marine Corps from the first day. Although he had never been much of an athlete in school, he found that the tough physical training in the Marines suited him perfectly. He also thrived on the discipline and the general atmosphere of the Marines, who prided themselves on being not only the toughest but also the brightest and the best. Ollie returned to Brockport State that fall, but it was clear to his classmates that the teacher's life was not for Ollie North.

At this point another Brockport student told Ollie that his father, Glenn Warner, was one of the athletic coaches at the Naval Academy at Annapolis. Would Ollie like to meet him? Ollie would indeed, because the Marines, after all, were a division of the Navy. It was through this meeting that Ollie was eventually able to arrange an appointment to Annapolis by one of New York's Republican congressmen, J. Ernest Wharton.

Oliver North started on a successful first, or plebe, year at the Naval Academy, but in February of 1964 he and several other plebes were in an automobile accident while on brief holiday leave over the weekend of Washington's Birthday. Their rented car collided with a trailer truck, killing one of the plebes and seriously injuring the others. Ollie suffered a broken nose and an injured back and right knee. The knee injury proved the most serious, eventually requiring two operations to repair damaged cartilage and leaving some doubt as to whether Ollie would be able to continue his naval career.

Young North returned home for the rest of that scholastic year and spent most of his waking hours exercising to regain full use of his right leg. A neighbor later told of seeing Ollie strengthening the leg by making jumps from the roof of his family home.

Returning to Annapolis, North was required to start over as a plebe. But he was able to convince Academy doctors of the full rehabilitation of his knee and was permitted to take part in intramural sports. And during Academy vacations Ollie did not go home but enrolled for further training in parachute jumping at Fort Benning, Georgia, and survival training in Nevada.

North graduated from Annapolis at about the middle of his class on June 5, 1968. He then immediately went to the Marine base at Quantico, Virginia, where he had to undergo five more months of basic infantry training. With the war in Vietnam now fully under way North was determined to get to that theater of war and earn awards and decorations that would at least match those that his father had earned in World War II. His only fear was that the war in Vietnam would be over before he could get there.

Before leaving for Vietnam Oliver North married Frances Elizabeth "Betsy" Stuart, a graduate of Pennsylvania State University. North had been introduced to Betsy by a cousin some months earlier. They were married on November 13, 1968, in a military ceremony at Quantico, honeymooned briefly in Puerto Rico, and then North was off to the war in Vietnam.

Second Lieutenant Oliver North was greatly respected by the enlisted men who served under him in combat. One of his men said that he gave orders from the front, not the rear; that is, he led his men into battle and didn't follow behind them where it was safer. North's brother officers, however, were somewhat skeptical about him. Several thought he was too "gung ho," too eager to charge into battle when a certain amount of discretion and caution might be called for. Such "gung ho" types too often caused unnecessary casualties, although they were the stuff from which heroes were made. Lt. North made no bones about the fact that he was after promotion and medals. He knew that combat provided the quickest way to gain military glory, so now that combat was readily available he meant to take advantage of it. But there were those who served with him who resented his risking their lives along with his own.

In the end North got what he had come to Vietnam for—medals and promotion. For valor and wounds suffered on the battlefield he was awarded the Silver Star, the Bronze Star, two Purple Hearts, and the Navy Commendation Medal. His wounds included broken ribs, a punctured lung, and shrapnel damage to his back and legs. Before he was returned to the United States in November 1969 North was promoted to First Lieutenant. Back at Quantico Oliver continued to seek promotion, but he did not make Captain until 1971. Meanwhile, his wife Betsy had given birth to two children—a daughter, Tait, and a son, Stuart. The family lived in inadequate dormitorylike housing on the Marine base at Quantico, where North was an instructor.

In 1973, North received orders to be transferred to the island of Okinawa, where he was to join a Marine amphibious, or ship-to-shore, landing team for training. He had to leave his family in the rude Quantico quarters less than two weeks before Christmas and was gone for a year. Apparently, being left alone yet once again and having to rear a fatherless family suddenly became too much for Betsy North. She wrote her husband in Okinawa telling him he could stay there as far as she was concerned and that she was taking their children and leaving.

Somehow this rift was repaired, but when North returned to the United States in 1974 he suffered a brief nervous breakdown. This attack was blamed on his marital problems. He was hospitalized for three weeks but was seemingly as good as new when he returned to duty. Later North claimed that all reference to this incident was removed from his military records so it would not stand in the way of his climb up the military ladder. His next assignment was in the Manpower Division of Marine Headquarters in Washington, D.C. North was not eager to become a "chairborne commando," but he knew that some desk duty was needed for career purposes. On July 1, 1978, North was promoted to Major.

In 1980, Major North received a plum assignment when he was chosen to attend the Naval War College at Newport, Rhode Island. He was graduated from there the following year. Graduates of the Naval War College were frequently assigned for three years of duty in Washington with the National Security Council. North thought he was already gaining too much of a reputation as a "desk jockey" and sought an assignment with troops in the field. Despite his desire in this matter Major North was assigned to the NSC.

North's new boss was Deputy National Security Adviser Robert C. McFarlane. Several years North's senior, McFarlane was an ex-Marine medal winner. Together the two Marine veterans would soon make national and even international headlines as they became entangled in the web of dealing arms-for-hostages and the Iran-Contra affair.

Oliver North quickly proved himself to be extremely valuable not only to NSC Deputy Director Robert McFarlane (he would soon be made director) but also to President Reagan and most of the other members of the Reagan administration. So valuable did he become that when the three years of his assignment to the NSC staff were up McFarlane asked the Marine Corps to extend North's term of NSC duty. Reluctantly the Marines agreed to do so.

One of the main reasons North became so valuable was that he worked so hard. He took sixteen-hour days in stride, and he was never one to turn down a new assignment. Equally important to his ability to carry an enormous work load was North's dedicated anti-communist conviction. This was especially important to the administration's prime movers against the Sandinista regime in Nicaragua.

The NSC was called upon to take over more and more of the anti-Sandinista efforts after the U.S. Central Intelligence Agency (CIA), headed by William Casey, overreached itself in Nicaragua. This false move by the CIA consisted of mining Nicaragua's harbors to prevent the flow of Soviet arms and other supplies into the country. Although the harbor-mining efforts were thought to have been secretly carried out, when the mines were discovered the United States was quickly identified as their source and the CIA was identified as the actual mine-laying organization. Since mining another country's harbors is clearly an act of war, both the Sandinistas and the U.S. Congress were angered by the irresponsible act, and the CIA had to reduce its Nicaraguan activities. Into this breech rode the NSC with Marine Major Oliver North leading the charge.

McFarlane and North gravitated toward one another more or less naturally. Like North, McFarlane had graduated from Annapolis and had also served in combat during a war. Although McFarlane was six years older than North, his war had also been in Vietnam, where he was decorated and rose to the rank of Lieutenant Colonel. After the war he served in several somewhat obscure Washington posts before being assigned to the NSC staff. He had resigned from the Marines to become the NSC deputy director.

McFarlane took North under his wing and proceeded to shelter and teach him how to deal in the politics of Washington. Dealing with a Congress that was especially reluctant to grant the Reagan administration a free hand in Central America was the main problem.

Interestingly, McFarlane, like North, had had an extremely demanding father who was also extremely patriotic. A Texas congressman, the elder McFarlane had instilled in his son a sense of dedication to his country and his government. Unlike North, however, young Robert McFarlane had grown up without the loving influence of a mother. His mother had died when Robert was eight, and he was reared by a stern and devout housekeeper. This influence almost led the boy to study for the ministry, but he eventually chose the military instead. Having served two tours of duty in Vietnam, McFarlane came away from that disastrous war with what he described as "a profound sense of very intolerable failure" at the way the conflict ended. [2] In a sense his government service since then had been an attempt to remedy that failure.

Under McFarlane's guidance North soon adopted the Contra cause as his own. He took at face value President Reagan's declaration that the Contras were true "freedom fighters" who should be compared with America's own founding fathers. This appealed powerfully to superpatriot North. Soon he was named deputy director of the NSC's political and military affairs division and given special authority on Central American problems. This appointment was accompanied by his being promoted to the rank of Lieutenant Colonel in the Marine Corps. In mid-October of 1983 McFarlane was named NSC director. He selected Rear Admiral John M. Poindexter as his deputy. The three men, McFarlane, Poindexter, and North, subsequently worked closely together on many NSC matters.

By 1984 almost all of the covert or secret Nicaraguan activity was being funneled through North. McFarlane was having to spend more and more time at the White House with President Reagan, laying plans for an upcoming summit meeting with the Soviet Union, but he made it clear to North that it was up to him "to hold the resistance together, body and soul." [3] One of the ways this was done was to quietly persuade foreign governments who were friendly to the United States to contribute large sums of money for the purchase of supplies and war matériel. It was then up to North to get this matériel into Contra hands.

By this time North had engaged the services of retired U.S. Air Force Major General Richard Secord and Iranian-born Albert Hakim, now an American citizen. Both men were recommended to North by CIA Director Casey, and they were able to take over much of the activity formerly performed by the CIA. Their work included obtaining war matériel and actually delivering it to

Nicaragua. Secord labeled this effort Operation Enterprise. Soon it would tie in with Oliver North's Project Democracy.

But in the beginning much of the money for Enterprise—some $24 million—was obtained from Saudi Arabia. Later other nations, such as Taiwan, as well as private contributors swelled the Contra coffers. But it was not until North more or less stumbled into the money that could be made in the arms-for-hostages deals with Iran that a truly major source of Contra funds was discovered. Secord and Hakim immediately fell in with Oliver North's secret source of funding for Project Democracy. Among other things it meant they could personally reap some dealers' profits from the arrangement. They saw to it that secret bank accounts were opened in Switzerland. Here, the money could be deposited and drawn upon as the members of North's team desired. Theoretically all of this money was to go to the Contras, but according to testimony later given by Contra leaders, much of it did not.

North shared his secret project with Admiral Poindexter. Just why he did not also share information about it with McFarlane until it had been going on for many months has never been clear. Perhaps it was because North thought McFarlane would not approve of it, despite his order to North that the Contra cause be kept alive at all costs. In any event, McFarlane did not learn of the diversion of arms-for-hostage funds to the Contras until his and North's failed trip to Tehran.

While operations Enterprise and Democracy were getting into high gear the United States found itself involved in two other acts of terrorism in the Middle East. Once again hostages were involved. In June of 1985, Shiite Party of God terrorists hijacked TWA flight 847 over Greece and subjected some 135 passengers to 17 days of nightmarish captivity. During this ordeal, in which the captive plane and its passengers were flown to several airports, one hostage, U.S. Navy diver Robert Dean Stethem, was shot and killed and his body brutally dumped on the runway at Beirut airport.

The TWA terrorists demanded the release of prisoners held by Israel in exchange for the plane's passengers. When Israel refused to negotiate, Syria stepped in and managed to persuade the hijackers to surrender. No additional passengers were harmed, but no action was taken against the terrorists.

That fall, on October 7, an Italian cruise ship, the *Achille Lauro*, was hijacked in Egyptian territorial waters. These hijackers, members of the Palestine Liberation Organization (PLO), also demanded the release of Israeli-held prisoners. Once again the Syrians managed to gain the release of the ship and its passengers but not before one of the Americans on board, Leon Klinghoffer, was assassinated. A wheelchair-bound invalid, Klinghoffer was brutally shot and his body thrown overboard.

Again no action was taken against the murdering hijackers. The United States attempted to get them extradited for trial in an American court but local authorities refused to turn them over.

All in all more than five hundred Americans died from acts of terrorism in the 1980s. This included some thirty-three people who were killed in April 1983 when a terrorist bomb exploded in the American embassy in Beirut, Lebanon. And in October of the same year, 241 U.S. Marines were killed in Beirut when several Iran-backed Lebanese fanatics drove trucks loaded with dynamite into the barracks of the Marines stationed there. The remaining Marines were withdrawn from the city, and Khomeini announced the murderous incident as yet one more victory over the "Great Satan"—America.

It is little wonder, therefore, that President Reagan

and his aides looked upon any even partially successful efforts against Khomeini and Iran with great favor. Up to this point Oliver North seemed to be the only person who had shown any hostage results whatsoever, and in addition he had greatly aided the Contra cause in Nicaragua. Nevertheless, when the arms-for-hostages deals and the method used to secretly fund the Contras became public knowledge, somebody had to take the blame since both activities were certainly unethical and probably illegal and unconstitutional.

OPERATION DAMAGE CONTROL

Despite the failure of the McFarlane-North mission to Tehran, several more arms deals with Iran were made before the lid was blown off the affair in the United States. To calm the public criticism, President Reagan called Oliver North to the White House, told him he was "a national hero"—and fired him. [1] The president also relieved Admiral Poindexter of his job as National Security Adviser.

Meanwhile, Attorney General Edwin Meese had been instructed to conduct a full investigation of the affair. He was authorized to do so by President Reagan, who apparently failed to indicate that there was any need for haste. In any event, Meese conducted a leisurely investigation, so leisurely that North had ample opportunity to remove most of the potentially damaging information about the arms-for-hostages deals from his office files. The telltale letters and memorandums were destroyed by putting them through a shredding machine. North's secretary, Fawn Hall, helped North in this "shredding party," as they dubbed it. In addition, Ms. Hall even carried some of the papers out of the office building by concealing them in her clothing. Poindexter had kept most of his pertinent information on computers, so he spent the time thoughtfully left available to him by Meese by clearing the NSC computers of all information about the Iran-Contra dealings.

During the course of his leisurely investigation Meese did manage to find one potentially incriminating piece of information that North had apparently missed in his file-clearing efforts. This was a memo that dealt with the diversion of federal funds from the arms sales to the Contras. Meese knew he must alert the president to the presence of this memo. Reagan's initial response was that he knew nothing about such an arrangement.

Reagan and his aides apparently thought that the heat from the Iran-Contra revelation would die down. When it did not, Reagan appointed a commission made up of both Republicans and Democrats to investigate and make public all of the details they could discover about the affair. The commission was made up of John Tower, a former Texas Senator and chairman of the Senate Armed Services Committee; Brent Scowcroft, a former National Security Adviser under President Gerald Ford; and Edmund S. Muskie, former Maine Senator and President Jimmy Carter's secretary of state.

The Tower Commission first met on December 1, 1986. Although its members worked steadily and hard, they were not able to deliver their findings until February 26, 1987. While the Tower Commission was carrying on its private investigation, Attorney General Meese also appointed an independent counsel or prosecutor, Lawrence E. Walsh, to carry on an investigation for the Justice Department. And finally another Iran-Contra investigation was conducted by a joint Congressional committee headed by Senator Daniel K. Inouye of Hawaii and Representative Lee H. Hamilton of Indiana.

When the Tower Commission issued its report, it dealt severely with both President Reagan and several members of the National Security Council. In criticizing President

Reagan the report said that the president had failed to control his staff or to understand exactly what it was they were doing. The report also made these accusations: Robert McFarlane had failed to keep the presidential Cabinet informed about the arms-for-hostages deals as well as the transfer of funds to the Contras. No acknowledgment was made of the fact that McFarlane had probably not found out about the illegal transfer of funds until long after this practice had begun. Admiral Poindexter, McFarlane's successor, had likewise failed to keep the Cabinet informed and had in addition lied to the Congress. Reagan's response to the report was his continued assertion that he had had no knowledge of the transfer of funds.

Other important events were also occurring in Washington during this period of turmoil. Frank C. Carlucci, a former intelligence officer, was named National Security Adviser to replace Poindexter. CIA Director William Casey was stricken with brain cancer and died in May of 1987. Earlier that year McFarlane was rushed to the hospital suffering from an overdose of sedative pills in what was said to be an attempt to commit suicide. He recovered.

McFarlane's despondency may have been brought on by the long and difficult interrogation he was subjected to by the secret Tower Commission hearings and the fact that he would probably have to face an equally difficult public grilling before the forthcoming congressional Iran-Contra hearings. But McFarlane was not to be the star of the joint congressional hearings, which lasted from May 5 to August 3 of 1987. Instead, his former aide, Lt. Col. Oliver North, took center stage at these hearings and, with the television lights and cameras full on him, became something of a popular sensation.

Each day that he testified at these hearings, Oliver

North made a point of appearing in full uniform and with all of his service ribbons decorating his chest. Sitting ramrod straight, he gave the impression of a superpatriotic young American who had been doing nothing more than serving his president, his country, and the Marines in the Iran-Contra affair. Making such statements as, "If the Commander in Chief tells this Lt. Col. to go stand in the corner and sit on his head, I will do so."[2] North was generally regarded among TV viewers as the personification of the hero Reagan had once claimed him to be. Co-chairmen Hamilton and Inouye tried to point out that North may well have been breaking the law and shredding the Constitution by running a separate, unelected government within a government, but their words seemed to have little effect on the public.

During the course of his testimony, however, North did admit he had lied along the way. This was necessary, he said, because sometimes it was essential to choose between "lies and [saving] lives."[3] This sort of witty response won North additional fans.

North's secretary, Fawn Hall, was also an attractive witness. She too displayed little sense of remorse over the misdeeds she may have committed in helping her boss steal classified documents and in shredding other vital material. At one point in her testimony she said, "Sometimes you have to go above the written law."[4]

Retired General Secord and Iranian expatriate businessman Hakim, North's partners in operations Enterprise and Democracy, also testified, Hakim making it clear that he regarded the several millions of dollars they had cleared as plain business profit. Others who testified included Assistant U.S. Secretary of State Elliot Abrams, who also admitted having lied in earlier testimony; Robert McFarlane; Admiral Poindexter; Contra leader Adolfo Calero, who insisted his forces had received nowhere near the millions of dollars that had apparently been cleared in the arms-for-hostages deals; Secretary of State Shultz; Defense Secretary Weinberger; chief of staff for the White House, Donald T. Regan; and Attorney General Meese.

North insisted that he assumed but could not prove that President Reagan had known of the diversion of Iranian funds. He also said that he had shredded documents because the late Bill Casey of the CIA had told him to do so. Accused of using Iran-Contra funds personally, North insisted he had simply been reimbursing himself for money he had already advanced. He did, however, admit accepting the gift of a security system for his home, although he tried to cover up this transaction with faked predated invoices marked "Paid." Arrangements had also been made, North claimed, for him to be the "fall guy" who would take the blame if knowledge of the Iran-Contra affair became public.

Most of Admiral Poindexter's testimony was hidden behind "can't remember" and "can't recall." He did admit that "the buck had stopped with him," that he purposefully withheld information from President Reagan about dealing with the Contras in order to provide the president with "deniability."[5]

It was clear that the joint congressional committee members did not believe all that they heard from the witnesses or accept all of the excuses. Co-chairman Lee Hamilton went so far as to say: "As I understand your testimony, you did what you did because . . . you believed it was for a good cause. I cannot agree that the end has justified these means, that the threat in Central America was so great that we had to do something, even if it meant disregarding Constitutional processes, deceiving the Congress and the American people. The means employed were a profound threat to the democratic process. . . . Methods and means are what this country are all about. We subvert our democratic process to bring about a desired end, no matter how strongly we may believe in that end. We've weakened our country and we have not strengthened it. A few do not know what is better for Americans than Americans know themselves. If I understand our government correctly, no small group of people, no matter how . . . well-intentioned they may be, should be trusted to determine policy."[6]

When the joint congressional committee finally issued its report in November of 1987 it stated flatly that President Reagan had to bear ultimate responsibility for the Iran-Contra affair. The committee stated that the President allowed several aides to make important foreign policy decisions while shirking his constitutional responsibility of making sure that the laws of the land were faithfully followed. The report, however, did not allege that any government officials actually committed any crimes. Nor did it accuse Reagan of knowing about the diversion of funds. Nevertheless, Lawrence E. Walsh, the independent counsel or prosecutor, began to push for criminal indictments against several of those named in the congressional report. A federal grand jury was convened to consider the issuing of such indictments. A federal grand jury examines accusations against persons charged with a federal crime or crime against the government and issues bills of indictment if the evidence warrants doing so. An indictment is simply an official charge of an offense.

Several statements made by the joint congressional committee could have acted as virtual outlines for indictments. One of these statements said, "The covert action was carried out in violation of the congressional notice provisions of the National Security Act."[7] Specifically, the Contra covert operation was carried out in violation of the country's public policy as expressed in the Boland Amendment restricting military aid to the Contras, and the Iran covert operation was carried out in violation of the country's stated policy against selling arms to Iran or making concessions to terrorists. Another said that these risky ventures were kept secret from Congress and Cabinet members who had voiced reservations and that secrecy was used to justify lies to Congress, the attorney general, and other Cabinet officers.

On Wednesday, March 16, 1988, several grand jury indictments were handed down in Washington, D.C. Indicted were Oliver North, John Poindexter, Richard Secord, and Albert Hakim. They were charged with conspiracy to defraud the United States, theft of government property, and other crimes. All four defendants pleaded not guilty.

Robert McFarlane was not indicted. Instead he pleaded guilty to four counts of withholding information from Congress, merely a misdemeanor, not a felony. The difference between the two kinds of misconduct is debatable, but a felony is always far more serious than a misdemeanor, which frequently results in nothing more than a short, suspended sentence. This reduced charge was allowed when McFarlane agreed to testify against the first of the accused to go on trial, his former aide, Lt. Col. Oliver North.

(Top) Anti-American demonstrators surround the United States Embassy in Tehran, Iran, shortly after the compound was seized. (Bottom) Iranian captors parade several blindfolded American hostages.

Ayatollah Ruhollah Khomeini (1900–1989)

Shah Mohammed Reza Pahlavi poses with his wife, the Empress Farah Diba, his oldest son, the Crown Prince Reza (far right), and other children.

Iranian Prime Minister Mohammed Mossadegh, known for his nationalist views, was ousted from power in a CIA-sponsored uprising.

(Above) Iranian officials examine documents captured in the aborted American rescue mission, Operation Eagle Claw. (Right) Secretary of State Cyrus Vance, who opposed the military mission to free American hostages in Iran, resigned his post in protest.

Like his predecessors, President Jimmy Carter was an ally of the Shah (right). He ended his term unable to resolve the hostage crisis.

President Ronald Reagan began his presidency by welcoming home the fifty-two freed American hostages.

*Pro-Iranian Shiite Muslims chant anti-U.S. slogans
as they burn effigies of Ronald Reagan (center), George
Shultz, and Israeli Prime Minister Yitzhak Shamir.*

Hatred of the West has led to acts of terrorism (clockwise, from top left): Rescuers scour the debris for victims after terrorists bombed the U.S. Marine barracks in Beirut; an armed Shiite Party of God terrorist stands guard during the hijacking of TWA flight 847, which resulted in the fatal shooting of a twenty-three-year-old U.S. Navy diver; Leon Klinghoffer's widow mourns over her husband's coffin. Klinghoffer was killed aboard the hijacked cruise liner Achille Lauro.

*President Reagan (center)
and John Poindexter
(right) look on as Robert
McFarlane announces
his resignation as
National Security
Adviser.*

*The president (center) chats with the Tower Commission he
appointed to investigate secret dealings with Iran and
Nicaraguan Contras. From left are: Secretary of State
George Shultz, John Tower, Edmund Muskie, and Brent
Scowcroft. Shultz was not a member of the Tower Commission.*

Ex-Iranian arms dealer Manucher Ghorbanifar (center) proposed an arms-for-hostages deal with Iran, using Israel as a third party. He is pictured here with arms dealer Adnan Khashoggi and ABC newswoman Barbara Walters.

Albert Hakim (left) and Richard Secord ran Operation Enterprise, which supervised the delivery of war matériel to Nicaraguan Contras.

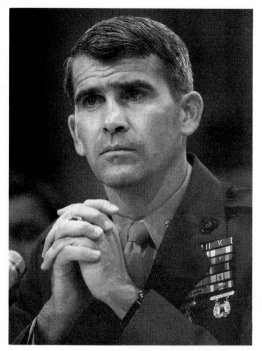

Marine Lt. Col. Oliver North

Senator Daniel Inouy (standing) administers the oath to Col. North (back to camera) on the first day of North's testimony during the Iran-Contra congressional hearings.

(Left) Fawn Hall, North's former secretary, testifies during the Iran-Contra hearings. (Below) Demonstrators from the Contragate Watch organization challenge the popular notion that Col. North is a great patriot.

of terrorism. You have discussed the general outlines of the Israeli plan with Secretaries Shultz and Weinberger, Attorney General Meese and Director Casey. The Secretaries do not recommend you proceed with this plan. Attorney General Meese and Director Casey believe the short-term and long-term objectives of the plan warrant the policy risks involved and recommend you approve the attached Finding. Because of the extreme sensitivity of this project, it is recommended that you exercise your statutory prerogative to withhold notification of the Finding to the Congressional oversight committees until such time that you deem it to be appropriate.

Recommendation

OK   NO

  — That you sign the attached Finding.

Prepared by:
Oliver L. North

Attachment
    Tab A - Covert Action Finding

1100 17 Jan 3.

President was briefed verbally from this paper. VP, Don Regan and Don Fortier were present.

JP

In a finding released by the White House, President Reagan's initials can be seen under the word "OK." Also, the handwritten line reads: "President was briefed verbally from this paper. VP [Bush], [chief of staff] Don Regan, and [National Security Council Adviser] Don Fortier were present." The line is initialed by John Poindexter.

National Security Adviser John Poindexter became the first Iran-Contra defendant to receive a prison sentence for his role in the cover-up.

NEW-HOSTAGE

A political cartoon illustrates how the Middle East hostage crisis has plagued three U.S. presidents.

(Above) Indian hostage Mithileshwar Singh (far left) and three American hostages—(left to right) Robert Polhill, Jesse J. Turner, and Alann Steen—appear in a photograph issued by their kidnappers. (Right) Freed U.S. priest Lawrence Jenco (right) accompanied here by Church of England envoy Terry Waite, ended his eighteen months as a hostage in July 1986.

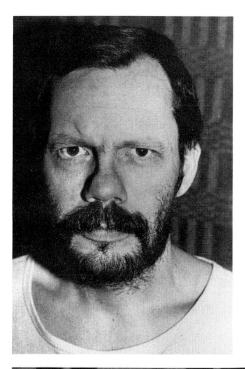

Three kidnapped U.S. hostages (clockwise from top left): Associated Press correspondent Terry Anderson, U.S. Marine Lt. Col. William Higgins, and CIA station chief in Beirut, William Buckley. Higgins and Buckley died in captivity.

Khomeini's portrait looms behind the new president of Iran, Ali Akbar Hashemi Rafsanjani.

President George Bush, shown here with newly released hostage Robert Polhill (left), has called for the unconditional surrender of all remaining American hostages.

OLIVER NORTH AND JOHN POINDEXTER GO TO TRIAL

Even before North went to trial his lawyer, Brendan Sullivan, began waging a strong campaign to have the most serious charges against the former National Security Council staff member dropped. Sullivan asked U.S. District Court Judge Gerhard Gesell to dismiss the charges of conspiracy and theft of government property against North. He based his request on the fact that to defend himself against these charges the ex-marine might have to disclose highly classified government information. He might, for example, make public secret cable communications between McFarlane and/or North and various Iranian officials. In addition he might be forced to disclose the names of CIA agents in the Middle East and Central America, and if these agents were identified, they might be killed. At the very least their future use would be jeopardized.

North and his lawyer were supported in their request by the federal Classified Information Act. This Act, passed during the Reagan Administration, was designed for use by the government in protecting secrets. Many U.S. lawmakers objected to the Act on the grounds that it enabled the executive branch of the government to carry on any kind of covert or secret operation it wanted to with no responsibility or accountability to Congress. To answer this objection, the president was required to issue what was called a "finding" to Congress giving the details of any particular covert activity. The only flaw in the "finding" requirement was that the president was supposed to issue such a statement "within a reasonable length of time" after a covert activity had begun. A chief executive who wanted to keep a covert activity truly secret could, of course, interpret "a reasonable length of time" to extend for days, weeks, or months.

Both Judge Gesell and special prosecutor Lawrence Walsh were most reluctant to drop or reduce any charges against North since some twenty-five months and $13 million had been spent in investigating North's role in the alleged illegal diversion of profits from the Iranian arms sales to the Nicaraguan Contras. One of the reasons a special prosecutor had been appointed was to allow him to spend all of his time concentrating on just this one case. Walsh had done just that and had come up with many pounds of evidence on paper to aid the prosecution. But this aid would have to come in the form of secret government documents. Consequently, when the Attorney General, Richard L. Thornburgh, who had replaced Meese, said flatly that the Reagan administration would not let North use any classified documents in his defense, the most serious charges against him were indeed dropped. Prosecutor Walsh said, however, he would proceed with the rest of the case against North. In his role as special prosecutor, Walsh was somewhat like a district attorney in a state court and had wide freedom of choice. But he was hemmed in severely by the federal control over vital evidence.

One of the most difficult problems in the North trial was in selecting a jury made up of members who claimed they had not been prejudiced one way or the other by the reports of the Tower Commission or the 1987 joint congressional hearings. There was some question about whether or not North could get a fair trial before jurors who had already formed opinions about his guilt or innocence before they tried him. In this instance prospective jurors had to insist they had not listened to or read about the earlier hearings if they were even to be considered as jurors in the North trial. After lengthy wrangling, a jury was finally sworn in and the trial began in February 1989.

Because of the restrictions regarding the admission of evidence, the North trial was inconclusive. North's main defense was that his actions had all been approved by Reagan, McFarlane, Poindexter, and Casey. Since Reagan indicated he would not testify, he was not asked to do so. McFarlane and Poindexter defended North but neither attempted to prove that Reagan had known about all of North's activities. Former CIA Director Casey was dead, so no testimony could be given by him. In a major sense Casey's testimony might well have been the most interesting of all. There was little doubt that the CIA Director had encouraged North in his early attempts to get hostages released in Lebanon. Casey's interest in these hostages had centered around the CIA station chief in Beirut, William Buckley. It was finally learned that Buckley had probably been tortured to death, a fact that was reported on October 4, 1985, but Casey continued to seek evidence about how much secret information Buckley may have disclosed before his death.

The important point that North and his lawyer did evidently manage to get across during the trial was that the ex-Marine had actually been a mere pawn in what he himself described as a "chess game played by giants." In fact, after the trial one juror, Earl Williams, told reporters: "I think there were people higher up who gave him the authority to do a lot of things, and then when he got caught out there high and dry, no one came to help him." And jury forewoman Denise Anderson went so far as to say, "North was the subordinate. He wasn't the boss. He wasn't running the show."[1]

The trial lasted until early May, and the jury took twelve days to reach a verdict. When the verdict finally came down it proved to be a partial victory for both sides. North was found guilty of illegally accepting the gift of the $13,800 home security system from General Secord and paid for out of Iran arms sale funds. He was also found guilty of trying to conceal the Iran-Contra scandal from Congress after the affair became public knowledge. But he was found not guilty on four counts of lying to Congress and one count of obstructing a congressional inquiry. Finally he was found guilty of altering, concealing, and shredding certain National Security Council documents. But he was found not guilty of the improper conversion of traveler's checks and conspiracy to defraud the United States and the Internal Revenue Service.

Judge Gesell set June 23 as the date on which to sentence North. His sentence, when it was handed down, was about as inconclusive as the trial verdict. North was placed on probation for two years and fined $150,000. The judge also gave the former NSC aide suspended sentences of three, two, and one years for North's three felony convictions. Later Judge Gesell said that the reason he had dealt comparatively lightly with North was because he did not want to make North a martyr and thus encourage continued hero worship on the part of his admirers.

"Your punishment will not include jail," the judge said. He added that he was not convinced that North appreciated what he had done wrong, but he was afraid "jail would only harden your misconceptions."[2]

In addition North was ordered to perform 1,200 hours

of community service and barred from ever again holding public office.

There were North supporters who thought even this mild sentencing was too severe and that the fine of $150,000 was excessive. Their minds were soon set at rest by reports that North had gone on the lecture circuit and was earning an estimated $200,000 a month by delivering two speeches a week at $25,000 per speech. As long as the lecture fees held out, it didn't seem likely that it would be necessary to hold any charity benefits for Oliver North.

In late 1989, two other Iran-Contra defendants, General Richard Secord and Iranian expatriate Albert Hakim, accepted a plea bargain, confessing to less serious crimes and promising to cooperate with the government in other Iran-Contra matters in exchange for lighter sentences. Secord admitted that he had lied to congressional investigators about what happened to the money from the Iran arms sales. Hakim pleaded guilty to the misdemeanor of helping to buy the security fence for Oliver North's suburban Washington home. Hakim also agreed to abandon his claim to most of Project Democracy's nine million dollars, that were frozen in Swiss bank accounts. In return for sparing the government a long and costly legal battle, Hakim was permitted to claim a share of the $1.7 million proceeds that could not be directly traced to the arms sales. Both men were placed on two years' probation, and Hakim was fined $5,000. Felony charges against them were dropped.

That left the highest-ranking Iran-Contra defendant still facing trial: former National Security Adviser John Poindexter. In setting the trial date for March 1990, U.S. District Court Judge Harold H. Greene rejected motions to dismiss charges against the retired admiral similar to those that had been thrown out when North was tried. Because he was accused of destroying documents and deceiving congressional committees by giving them doctored chronologies and misleading information, Poindexter faced five counts of conspiracy, obstructing Congress, and making false statements. Like the other Iran-Contra defendants, he was being held accountable for the Iran-Contra coverup, deceiving Congress, and not for the sale of arms to Iran or the diversion of funds to Nicaragua.

Poindexter's defense lawyers, led by Richard W. Beckler, requested notes and diaries kept by former President Reagan in the hope of proving that their client had acted under orders and with the president's full knowledge. In pretrial comments to the press, Judge Greene said one of the excerpts included an entry that included "a somewhat ambiguous comment arguably indicating that the former President knew of the defendant's actions on behalf of the Contras."[3] On a number of these issues, it is claimed, President Reagan formulated the administration's position for guidance of Poindexter and sometimes others. On other issues Mr. Reagan allegedly entertained Poindexter's plans without voicing any objections.[4] The judge ordered the former president to turn over the written materials to him.

Reagan's lawyers objected to the order on the grounds of executive privilege, the right of the executive branch to withhold confidential information from Congress and the courts. Although executive privilege is not mentioned in the Constitution, the Supreme Court recognized the president's limited right to invoke the legal doctrine in the 1974 case of *United States* v. *Richard M. Nixon*. Consequently, Judge Greene reviewed 100 diary entries in private and ruled in favor of the former president. He explained that the notations did not shed any new light on the Iran-Contra affair so they were not required as evidence.[5]

Judge Greene did uphold Poindexter's lawyers when

they subpoenaed Mr. Reagan, compelling the former president to testify at the trial. Greene reasoned that Reagan had been the national security adviser's immediate superior. Unlike Oliver North, further down the chain of command, Poindexter was therefore entitled to have his lawyers question the president about his knowledge of the affair. The judge permitted a presidential deposition to be taken on videotape for use at the trial.

Dressed in a dark business suit, Mr. Reagan seated himself in the witness box of a Los Angeles courtroom and submitted to questioning by Poindexter's lawyers and the prosecutors. He gave eight hours of taped testimony on February 16–17, 1990, to be presented at the actual trial. But his statements did little to support Poindexter's claims to be following presidential orders. Reagan did confirm that he had been involved in some aspects of the affair. He acknowledged that he had urged foreign heads of state to fund and equip the Contras.[6] But this added nothing new to what was already known.

Reagan's mind went blank when he was asked to recall specific meetings, dates, or memos. He failed to recognize two well-known Contra leaders after he was shown a photograph of them taken at the White House. He couldn't even remember that his once-trusted adviser Robert McFarlane had pleaded guilty to withholding information from Congress. Despite the well-publicized findings of the Tower Commission that arms sales to Iran had been diverted to the Contras, the former president insisted, "I had no knowledge then or now that there had been a diversion, and I never used the term."[7] As a potential defense witness, Reagan was more or less a failure.

The Poindexter trial opened on March 5, 1990, and lasted until April 7. Judge Greene examined prospective jurors and dismissed those who had prior knowledge of Iran-Contra events. He did not think that the ability to recognize the names of prominent figures in the affair was grounds for automatic disqualification. He also ruled that Oliver North would be permitted to testify for the prosecution on a wide range of Iran-Contra matters.

When North took the stand, he soon proved to be a hostile witness for chief prosecutor Dan K. Webb of the special prosecutor's office. But his testimony was damaging to Poindexter's case since he repeatedly said that he concealed nothing from his former superior and operated under the national security adviser's direction. On the second day of his testimony, North reluctantly admitted that he saw Poindexter destroy a presidential order authorizing secret arms sales, a key charge leveled against the retired admiral. Oliver North's secretary, Fawn Hall, followed him on the witness stand. She stated that she did not think Poindexter knew about North's directives to alter several classified documents about secret aid to the Contra rebels.[8] Then, two computer experts testified that Poindexter had gone to great lengths to destroy Iran-Contra documents, deleting more than 5,000 messages from his personal computer in late November 1986. The prosecution called a total of ten witnesses before completing its case. In marked contrast to the Oliver North trial, where the defense team kept the prosecution off balance, the Poindexter prosecutors managed to present a "disciplined and emotionally charged courtroom performance."[9]

Chief defense lawyer Beckler's strategy was to show that Poindexter operated under presidential directives and to prove that Congress was aware that funds had been diverted to the Contras. A total of fifteen witnesses testified for the defense, including a middle-level CIA agent, Illinois Republican congressman Henry J. Hyde, and Ronald Reagan, the last by videotape. Poindexter's attorneys presented summaries of classified documents claiming the House Intelligence Committee knew that the Contras were still receiving American aid in 1985, a time when such aid was no longer lawful. Summaries can be used in trials involving secret government activities. Government agents review them to make sure the relevant information is presented without compromising the government's security, and both the prosecution and defense stipulate that for purposes of the trial the summaries are accurate representations of the truth. Apparently the Bush administration was somewhat more flexible about classified data than the Reagan administration had been. Of course, outside the courtroom, Indiana Democrat Lee Hamilton, who had chaired the House Intelligence Committee in 1985, called the claim "fundamentally wrong."[10]

After less than six days of testimony, the defense rested its case. But Poindexter never took the stand. Chief defense lawyer Beckler told reporters that Poindexter's testimony was not needed, stating, "The Government didn't prove its case as far as I'm concerned."[11] Then, Judge Greene issued his instructions to the jury. He told them to ignore value judgments about the administration's policies toward Iran and Nicaragua and focus their attention instead on specific evidence of crimes "as distinct from broad policy" when they applied the law to the facts of the case."[12] He also advised them not to give any special weight to Reagan's testimony.

It took the jury six days to find John Poindexter guilty of all five charges against him. Chief defense lawyer Beckler announced to reporters that the jury's findings would be appealed to a higher court.

On June 11, John Poindexter became the first Iran-Contra defendant to receive a prison sentence. Judge Greene gave him a six-month jail term but did not impose a fine. The maximum penalty for Poindexter's five felony convictions was twenty-five years in jail and a $1.25 million fine. The sentence took into consideration the former national security adviser's role in the Iran-Contra cover-up as well as his impressive career as a naval officer with over thirty years of service to his country. Poindexter remained free pending his appeal. If the appeal failed, Poindexter would probably serve not more than three or four months of his sentence since he could earn time off for good behavior. [13]

Despite Poindexter's conviction, Special Prosecutor Walsh was determined to pursue the Iran-Contra inquiry further. [14] On May 18, a new federal grand jury opened a criminal investigation into the affair. It focused on the role played by middle-level Reagan administration officials. Meanwhile two public interest groups, the National Security Archive and the Public Citizen, had successfully sued the federal government under the Freedom of Information Act. They demanded that officials declassify and release portions of Oliver North's diaries and personal notes, previously withheld on grounds of national security. Publication of these materials in mid-May revealed that up to the time North was fired, he had been in communication with many important members of the Reagan administration, including Vice-President Bush, as well as with foreign leaders. It came as no surprise when the grand jury summoned North to testify at a closed hearing and granted him immunity from further prosecution. Poindexter also appeared as a witness. Perhaps, under the grand jury's scrutiny, lingering questions about the involvement of Ronald Reagan and George Bush in the Iran-Contra affair would finally be answered.

PRESIDENT BUSH FACES HIS OWN HOSTAGE CRISES

Like the Vietnam War, which tarnished the images of several U.S. presidents—John F. Kennedy, Lyndon Johnson, Richard Nixon—the hostage crisis in the Middle East either tarnished or threatened to tarnish several other U.S. chief executives—Jimmy Carter, Ronald Reagan, and finally George Bush.

As vice-president, Bush managed to avoid any major responsibility for the Iran-Contra scandal. A year after he succeeded Reagan as president, Bush had reason to hope that he might soon be rid of the Contra problem. In Nicaragua, Sandinista leader Daniel Ortega was voted out of power in an internationally supervised election on February 25, 1990. A coalition headed by Violeta Barrios de Chamorro took over the government. By mid-April, rebel army camps in Honduras were being dismantled. After the Contra and Sandinista leaders signed a cease-fire agreement, some of the guerrilla forces gradually demobilized.

But Bush also inherited the hostage problem, which was far from solved. And he had been in office only a few months when the problem once again reached a crisis stage. In the mid-summer of 1989, President Bush was in the middle of a political speaking engagement in Chicago when he received word that an American Marine officer who had been held hostage in the Middle East since February 17, 1988, had been murdered by his Hezbollah, or Party of God, Shiite captors. Bush immediately canceled the remainder of his scheduled trip and returned to Washington for consultation with his top military and foreign affairs aides.

The man assassinated was Marine Lt. Col. William R. Higgins, 44, who was the head of an observer group attached to the United Nations peacekeeping force. An especially brutal aspect of the Higgins execution was a videotape released by his captors showing Higgins's corpse twirling from the end of a rope, indicating the Marine officer had been hanged. There was some debate by experts over whether or not the videotape had been made recently or some months earlier, when Higgins had first been kidnapped. The experts were in agreement, however, that the body was indeed that of Colonel Higgins.

From the very beginning, in 1987, there had been controversy in the Marine Corps about Higgins's assignment to the peacekeeping force. Higgins had worked for Caspar Weinberger when Weinberger was Defense Secretary. In that job Higgins had seen virtually every classified document that Weinberger had seen. There were those who thought that a high-ranking Marine officer with Higgins's knowledge of classified information would make an ideal candidate for kidnapping by the Party of God. When just that happened in 1988 many Marines expressed their anger over the situation, a situation in which nothing really seemed to be being done. Now, with Higgins's murder, not only the Marines but other service people as well as civilians in government began to talk of the United States taking some sort of military action.

As soon as he reached the White House, President Bush asked the Defense Department to brief him on the attack-and-rescue operations that had tentatively been planned in the seventeen months since Higgins had been captured. After this meeting it would appear that nothing had been ruled out.

But apparently nothing had been ruled in either, for, eager as he was to take positive action in his first international crisis, Bush—like Carter and Reagan before him—was soon forced to realize that the superpower United States was all but helpless in the face of the hit-and-run tactics of the Middle East terrorists.

There was, of course, formidable and quickly available military power that Bush could call upon should he choose to use it. On routine patrol in the Mediterranean Sea were twenty-one U.S. Navy ships. One of these ships was the aircraft carrier *Coral Sea*, which could immediately launch jet fighters and bombers to attack targets in Lebanon.

If Bush were to order an invasion, there was also the so-called Amphibious Ready Group of 2,400 Marines aboard ships near the island of Crete. These troops were trained to storm beaches and attack military installations from helicopters.

Other naval forces in the nearby Mediterranean included guided-missile cruisers, frigates, destroyers, ammunition ships, oilers, helicopter carriers, and landing craft that could put Marines and tanks ashore. In addition, just off the coast of France was the U.S.S. *Iowa* with its powerful 16-inch guns that could shell an enemy's shores.

If a direct attack on Iran for its role in the Beirut hostage situation was decided upon, there were also some twenty naval vessels in the Persian Gulf, the Gulf of Oman, the Arabian Sea, and the Indian Ocean.

There were, however, certain questions that had to be answered if any military action was to be undertaken. First of all, did the United States know the specific group of terrorists responsible for Higgins's capture and murder? Could the location of this group be pinpointed? If military action was undertaken, could the attack be carried out without serious mass damage to the surrounding civilian population?

While the military planners were debating these questions an additional threat of further assassinations hung over the hostages' heads. Word was received from the Party of God leaders that unless a particular prisoner held by the Israelis was released, another American would be hanged. And the assassinations would continue until all of the hostages were dead. The particular person whose release was demanded by the terrorists was a Muslim cleric named Sheik Abdul Karim Obeid, who was one of the leaders of the Hezbollah. The Israelis had captured him in retaliation for several Israelis who were being held hostage.

Had the Party of God terrorists followed through with even one more assassination the United States probably would have resorted to the use of force in an attack of some kind. But while Bush and his aides were debating about what to do, the ruler of Syria, Hafez Assad, quietly moved in and apparently told the terrorists to withdraw their additional threats. When the deadline for killing another hostage came and passed without incident, it was clear that Assad's orders had been followed. Shortly afterward the Party of God announced that any further executions would be postponed.

Syria's Assad had long been a behind-the-scenes power in the Middle East. Syrian troops actually controlled much of Lebanon and were a constant threat to Israel. The long military siege under which Beirut had suffered was largely Syria's responsibility, although the Palestine Liberation Organization (PLO) under Yasir Arafat was a disruptive force in its efforts to seize some semblance of homeland in the region. Both Syria and the PLO were, of course, opposed by the Israelis, who feared their country would be wiped from the face of the earth if they lost any kind of war to their enemies in the region. As a result, Lebanon in general and Beirut in particular had become desolate battlegrounds after months and years of ceaseless guerrilla-type warfare.

The high-level debate in Washington either openly decided against taking any overt action in Lebanon following Higgins's death, or by silent mutual consent agreed against it. In any event no immediate action was taken. And when the Party of God called off any further assassinations, the Higgins affair gradually drifted into limbo as had most other events involving American hostages.

But gradually in the next several months the tempo of the destructive warfare in Beirut increased as an artillery war was waged by Syria against yet another foe. This was the so-called Lebanese Christian Army of General Michel Aoun, a splinter group that was trying to gain control of the area. As the Syrian bombardment of the Lebanese capital grew all through late 1989, the civilian population dwindled, not only from bombing casualties but also because of a general exodus from the city. Even with little or no place to go, the civilian population simply began to pour out of Beirut in a never-ending stream. Walking, riding bicycles, pushing wheeled carts bearing their few belongings, the people fled the daily terror of the guns. By now Beirut, which had once been one of the most beautiful cities in the Middle East, was a wasteland.

It was in the middle of this exodus, when Beirut gave indication of becoming a ghost city, that President Bush and the U.S. State Department decided to take drastic action. They decided to close the U.S. Embassy in Beirut to avoid the possibility of its becoming a second Tehran Embassy filled with American hostages held this time by the PLO or Syrians. The closing of an embassy is always regarded as an extreme diplomatic measure.

Whether or not this move was wholly justified, it certainly put at least a temporary halt to the taking of any more American hostages in the area. Bush had already told any Americans left in Lebanon to leave, and further travel into the area was discouraged. This did not, of course, solve the problem of the American hostages still left in Lebanon. In fact it cut back drastically any chance of dealing with the hostage problem in an immediate manner.

No hostages other than Higgins had been taken in 1988 or 1989. Four additional hostages, however, had been taken in 1987. Three men, all kidnapped on January 24, were Jesse J. Turner, 42, visiting assistant professor of mathematics and computer science at Beirut University College; Alann Steen, 50, journalism professor at Beirut University College; and Robert Polhill, 55, assistant professor of business and lecturer in accounting at Beirut University College. A fourth man, Charles Glass, was kidnapped on June 17. A former ABC correspondent in Beirut, where he was writing a book, Glass escaped on August 18, 1987.

Of the seventeen men taken hostage in Lebanon between 1984 and 1988, six were believed to have escaped or been released. These were Frank Reiger, Jeremy Levin, Rev. Benjamin F. Weir, Father Lawrence Martin Jenco, David P. Jacobsen, and Charles Glass. Three were believed to be dead. These were William Buckley, Peter Kilburn, and Marine Lt. Col. William Higgins. This left eight Americans who were believed to be still alive and in captivity in Lebanon when President Bush began his term in office. They were Terry A. Anderson, Thomas Sutherland, Frank H. Reed, Joseph J. Cicippio, Edward A. Tracy, Alann Steen, Jesse J. Turner, and Robert Polhill. In addition to these eight Americans, there were also eight hostages being held from other Western countries.

The eventual fate of these prisoners depended to a

considerable degree upon decisions that could be made by Iranian leaders who still had a powerful voice in Middle Eastern affairs. On June 3, 1989, the Iranian nation mourned the death of the Ayatollah Khomeini, who died from heart and intestinal disorders. Khomeini's successor as president of Iran, Ali Akbar Hashemi Rafsanjani, declared publicly, late in 1989, that if the United States would release the remaining several billion dollars in Iranian assets, frozen since 1979, his government would help win the release of Western hostages in Lebanon. Of course, the pragmatic Rafsanjani had to contend with hard-line fundamentalists who opposed any attempt to normalize relations with the West.

Like Carter and Reagan before him, Bush wanted nothing more than to get the current hostages released with the promise that no more would be taken. Bush realized full well that hostage-taking resulted in the United States itself—not just its citizens—being taken hostage and rendered powerless to act effectively against this terrorist practice. In his inaugural address, Bush had suggested to the Iranians that "good will begets good will."[1] In March 1990, the president repeated this message to a phone caller purported to be Mr. Rafsanjani. While Bush flatly insisted that neither he nor his aides would take part in hostage deals, he had often stated that he would talk to "anyone, anytime" to secure the release of the hostages. This time, he was the victim of a hoax. White House officials belatedly discovered that his caller was not the president of Iran nor anyone authorized to act on his behalf. In Tehran, Rafsanjani mocked Bush for his willingness to conduct diplomacy by telephone. But the president stuck by his policy of behind-the-scenes conversations rather than diplomacy by headlines.

Despite his public scorn of Bush's methods, for several months Rafsanjani had been conveying private messages to the president through the Japanese and Swiss embassies indicating that he wanted to improve relations with the United States.[2] Facing a troubled economy and increasing international isolation in the aftermath of the war with Iraq, Rafsanjani wanted to secure trade and aid agreements from the West in addition to the frozen assets. The Iranian government had been quietly putting pressure on the Lebanese to give up their hostages—even to the point of giving the Lebanese militants arms and funds to obtain the promise of a hostage release.[3]

Iranians were joined in this effort by Syria. President Assad was finding the costs of maintaining Syrian control over Lebanon an increasing drain on his nation's resources. He seemed eager to mend fences with his Arab neighbors and the West in view of slackening Soviet support.[4] Syria's influence over the hostage-takers had been limited by its ties to the Amal Shiites, secular opponents of the fundamentalist Party of God Shiites. But ever since a pro-Syrian leader had gained control of the hostages held by the Party of God, Syria had been able to restrain the excesses of the fundamentalists,[5] as was seen during the Higgins affair. Urged on by the United States, Assad was ready to take a more active role in the hostage situation. And it was rumored that there would soon be a break in the hostage standoff.

In mid-April, a Beirut newspaper published a handwritten letter from a Party of God splinter group and a recent photograph of hostage Jesse Turner. The group was also known to be holding Alann Steen and Robert Polhill. Crediting appeals from Iranian and Syrian officials, the group offered to release one of these three hostages as a "good will initiative" to help resolve the hostage situation.[6] One condition that the hostage-takers stipulated was that Assistant Secretary of State for Near Eastern Affairs John Kelly, former Ambassador to Lebanon, be sent to Syria to arrange the transfer. President Bush refused to comply, explaining that, "The United States does not give in to demands."[7] Referring to American ambassador to Syria Edward P. Djerejian, Bush noted that the United States had a "perfectly capable, accredited diplomat on the scene in Syria."[8]

In response, the terrorist group issued another statement, postponing the release. This time they included a snapshot of hostage Robert Polhill. By playing a waiting game, the Lebanese militants were able to focus world attention once again on themselves and on the Americans held captive in the Middle East. They sought to inflame public opinion and build up the hopes of the hostages' families so that Bush would be pressured into doing what they wanted. But the president held firm. He would make no concessions to terrorists.

After a suspenseful four-day wait, on April 22, Robert Polhill was turned over to Syrian intelligence officers. In preparation for his eventual return to the United States, he was driven to Damascus, Syria, where American diplomats awaited his arrival. Upon hearing of his release, President Bush thanked the Syrian government for making the arrangements. He commented that he did not know whether Iran had been directly involved and was grateful if indeed Iran had helped. When reporters asked him whether the United States would reciprocate, he told them, "I'm not making gestures. I don't trade for hostages."[9] With the Iran-Contra affair still fresh in the public's memory, Bush adamantly demanded that all of the remaining hostages be freed unconditionally. Only then would "good will beget good will." Rumors had circulated that a second hostage would be freed. But it did not help matters any that Congress chose this time to pass a nonbinding resolution recommending that a unified Jerusalem become the capital of Israel.

Nevertheless, on April 29, exactly one week after Mr. Polhill's safe return, a Beirut news agency received a statement from a previously unknown terrorist group and a photo of hostage Frank Herbert Reed. His captors promised to free him within forty-eight hours with a message for the American government. [10] The very next day, Reed was placed in the custody of the Syrian military, who brought him to the Foreign Ministry in Damascus, retracing the route recently taken by Robert Polhill. By now, Polhill was back in the United States after spending several days at a medical facility in Wiesbaden, West Germany. He was visiting the White House at the same time that Reed was being greeted by Syrian and American officials in Damascus.

At a welcoming ceremony for Polhill, President Bush pointedly expressed his appreciation to both the Syrian and Iranian governments for bringing about Reed's release. But he reminded the public that U.S. policy toward Iran and Syria had not changed and would not change unless and until all American hostages were returned. [11] The same day, as if to emphasize President Bush's comments, the State Department made public its annual report on states supporting terrorism, continuing to list Syria and Iran on the roster. Later, in a private meeting, Polhill delivered a message from his captors to the president. Its contents were not disclosed.

Iranian and Syrian sources indicated that other American hostages would be released if the United States were willing to make some concessions. In fact, several Iranian officials issued statements urging the United States to pressure Israel to exchange its Muslim captives for the remaining American and European hostages. At his press conference with Polhill, President Bush had stated that since he opposed all hostage-taking, he would have no objections to Israel's freeing their Shiite prisoners, but that was a decision for the Israeli government to make. As a humanitarian gesture, he did offer to find out what had happened to Iranians captured in 1982 by Lebanese Christian forces. American officials soon notified the Iranian government that these individuals had died in captivity.[12]

Some Middle East analysts argued that time was running out, that pragmatic Iranian officials might be replaced by uncompromising fundamentalists, less inclined to end the hostage standoff. Others maintained that even if the pragmatists stayed in power, it was unclear that they would continue to exert influence over the splinter groups of the Party of God much longer. These Lebanese terrorist organizations might insist on keeping their hostage bargaining chips until Shiites imprisoned in Kuwait and Israel were freed, and the groups were guaranteed immunity from retaliatory attacks from the United States, Syria, or Israel.[13]

The American people were not about to forget the hostages and abandon them to their fate. But they supported their president in his refusal to negotiate with the terrorists for the hostages' return. Whether Bush's policy prolonged or broke the hostage stalemate remained to be seen. At least, Polhill and Reed had been set free. Maybe others would follow.

Epilogue

As this book is being completed, the legacy of the hostage crisis and the Iran-Contra affair is still unfolding. In the Middle East, Party of God fundamentalists continue to hold fourteen American and Western European hostages. Brief articles in the American press have revealed that there was some movement to secure the release of Swiss captives. Indeed, in August 1990, two Swiss hostages were released into Syrian hands.

But the Iranians have shown little interest in helping to free the remaining Americans. After an earthquake devastated portions of Iran on June 21, 1990, Rafsanjani's spokespeople pointedly conveyed that American humanitarian aid in response to the disaster had no bearing on the ongoing hostage situation. The Iranians did not intend to pressure their cohorts in Lebanon to turn over any more Americans to the Syrians. Evidently, the United States had not met Iran's unannounced ransom for these captives. Whatever those stakes might be, President Bush has consistently held to his policy of refusing to negotiate with the hostage takers.

Further complicating the issue was the sudden show of force by the president of Iraq, Saddam Hussein. In August 1990, U.S. forces landed in Saudi Arabia in response to

Iraq's seizure of Kuwait and perceived threats to the Saudi kingdom. To prevent further military action on the part of Western powers and their Arab allies, the Iraqis are using Western foreign nationals in Kuwait and Iran as "hostages."

Such factors as Iran's enmity toward Iraq, and Arab ambivalence—if not hostility—toward the presence of American troops on Middle Eastern soil could further complicate an already volatile situation. On the other hand, there is an old expression to the effect that "an enemy of my enemy is my friend." Perhaps U.S. attempts to check Iraq's aggression would soften Iranian attitudes over the long run. Yet Iraq's efforts to raise world oil prices—even at the price of Kuwaiti independence— could benefit the troubled Iranian economy. So it is hard to predict what the ultimate impact of American intervention in the Middle East will be.

The effects of the Iran-Contra affair are still being felt. In Nicaragua, President Violeta Chamorro's fragile coalition government has withstood a Sandinista-endorsed labor strike. The Nicaraguan economy remains weak and prospects for long-term stability are uncertain.

In the United States the scandal has left a heritage of legal appeals. On July 20, 1990, a divided three-member panel assigned to reappraise whether or not Oliver North received a "fair trial" issued a ruling. The ruling overturned North's conviction for destroying government records on the grounds that two highly technical mistakes had been made in the judge's instructions to the jury. (The two Reagan appointees on the panel supported North's claims while the third judge had objected to their conclusions.)

What made the panel's findings controversial was the decision to send North's two remaining convictions back to Judge Gerhard Gesell because of the possibility that they resulted from testimony that the former Marine colonel had given before Congress. Eager to pinpoint responsibility for the Iran-Contra affair, Congress had granted North immunity, exempting him from prosecution for what he would say, in exchange for his testimony at the hearings. This way, witnesses can make sworn statements but be protected from incriminating themselves at criminal trials. Freedom from self-incrimination is guaranteed by the Fifth Amendment to the Constitution. Later, North's defense lawyers had argued that their client did not receive a fair trial because even though transcripts of his immunized testimony were not allowed to be presented to the jury, that testimony had been widely publicized. They claimed that North had been convicted because of what he had said before Congress and not because of evidence presented to the jury.

In a 1972 case, *Kastigar* v. *United States*, the Supreme Court had ruled that prosecutors must show that no evidence used in a trial was developed from immunized testimony. The three-judge panel that had heard North's appeal went even further and outlined the steps that prosecutors would have to take to prevent grand jurors and trial witnesses from being exposed to or aware of immunized testimony. Prosecutors found these steps virtually impossible to meet and wondered whether the panel's ruling would jeopardize the grand-jury investigation of the role that middle-level Reagan officials played in the Iran-Contra affair. There was also concern that Poindexter's five convictions would be overturned.

In the short run, the circuit court had left open the possibility that Oliver North could receive a new trial, provided additional precautions were taken to exclude immunized testimony. Alternatively, Special Prosecutor Lawrence Walsh could choose to appeal the North reversal before the full circuit court or take the case to the Supreme

Court. In the future, Congress would have to reconsider its policy of granting immunity to witnesses who face criminal proceedings, and the courts would have to refine trial procedures affecting witnesses who had given immunized testimony to protect their constitutionally guaranteed right to a fair trial. This is probably the most important effect of the Iran-Contra scandal.

An even more important issue seemed to be neglected during the debate over immunity—the issue of remedying abuses of power by executive branch staff members. Both Congress and the president owe the American public some guarantee that checks would be put in place to prevent staffers, however well intentioned, from exercising discretionary power and taking actions without clearly documented authorization from their superiors. Democratic government requires responsible leadership and obedience to law. Perhaps the scandal has served to remind Americans and their lawmakers once more that they must take measures to ensure that they continue to live under a government of laws and not a government of men. Whatever the outcome of all these developments, one thing is certain: Americans have not heard the last of the hostage crisis or the Iran-Contra affair.

CHRONOLOGY

AMERICAN HOSTAGES
IN LEBANON

PHOTOGRAPHY CREDITS

NOTES

BIBLIOGRAPHY

INDEX

CHRONOLOGY

1979

January 16   Shah leaves Iran.

February 1   Ayatollah Ruhollah Khomeini returns to Iran after 15-year exile to establish Islamic Republic.

November 4   Sixty-six American hostages are seized at U.S. Embassy, Tehran.

November 14   U.S. imposes embargo on arms shipments to Iran.

1980

April 7   U.S. severs diplomatic relations with Iran; exports to Iran banned; Iranian diplomats in U.S. expelled.

April 25   U.S. mission to rescue American hostages aborted in Iranian desert due to equipment failures.

April 26   Secretary of State Cyrus Vance resigns; succeeded by Maine Senator Edmund Muskie.

July 27	Shah dies in exile in Cairo, Egypt.
September 22	Iraq invades Iran.
November 4	Ronald Reagan elected U.S. president.

1981

January 20	Reagan inaugurated 40th president; George Bush inaugurated vice-president; Iran releases fifty-two U.S. captives seized at embassy in Tehran November 1979, 444 days after capture.
January 21	Jimmy Carter greets freed Americans, Wiesbaden, West Germany.
August	Lt. Col. Oliver North joins National Security Council after graduating from Naval War College.
December	Reagan authorizes covert CIA operation to support Contras in Nicaragua.

1982

June 25	Alexander Haig resigns as Secretary of State; George Shultz appointed.
December 21	First Boland Amendment signed into law.

1983

October 17	Robert C. McFarlane appointed National Security Adviser.
October 23	Two suicide terrorist trucks bomb the U.S. Marine and French military barracks in Beirut, killing 241 American and 56 French servicemen.
December 8	Second Boland Amendment signed into law; $24 million cap placed on military funds to Contras.

1984

Summer	Arms-for-Hostages idea formed.
July	Secord and North first discuss Contra aid; Secord arranges arms sales to Contras.
October 12	Third Boland Amendment signed into law.
November 6	Reagan re-elected president in greatest Republican landslide in history.

1985

June 14	TWA flight 847 hijacked.
June 30	TWA hostages released.
July 11	Hostage arms swap proposed.
Mid-July	McFarlane briefs Reagan on Iran.
Early August	Approval of Israeli sale to Iran.
August 17–30	Financing of arms deal.
October 7	American tourist, Leon Klinghoffer, killed by PLO terrorists aboard the hijacked cruiseship *Achille Lauro*.
December 4	Poindexter named to succeed McFarlane, who is resigning as National Security Adviser.

1986

January 7	Reagan and top advisers discuss Iran initiative; meeting includes Bush, Regan, Shultz, Weinberger, Casey, Meese, Poindexter.
February 25	Reagan requests Contra aid; asks Congress for $100 million in aid, including $70 million in military assistance.

May 25	North, McFarlane, and other officials meet with Iranians to win release of hostages.
June 26	House approves Reagan request for military aid to Contras by 221–209 vote.
October 30	Contra aid approved. Reagan signs into law bill appropriating $70 million in military aid and $30 million in nonmilitary aid.
November 3	*Al-Shiraa* discloses McFarlane's secret May trip to Tehran.
November 25	Poindexter resigns. North fired by Reagan for role in diverting funds to Contras.
November 28	Senate Committee on Intelligence announces it has begun to investigate the Iran-Contra affair.
December 1	Tower Commission established to review operations of National Security Council staff and to recommend reforms.
December 19	Lawrence E. Walsh selected independent counsel to investigate Iran-Contra affair.

1987

January 6	Senate Select Committee established.
January 7	House Select Committee established.
January 12	Frank C. Carlucci, successor to Poindexter, bars NSC staff from undertaking covert activities.
January 29	Senate Committee on Intelligence releases report.
February 2	CIA Director Casey resigns; Robert M. Gates nominated successor.

February 26	Tower Commission report released blaming Iran-Contra debacle on key White House staffers and Reagan.
February 27	White House Chief of Staff Regan resigns; former Senate majority leader Howard Baker, Jr., succeeds.
March 18	House and Senate Select Committees agree to hold joint hearing.
May 5	Joint hearings of House and Senate Select Committees begin.
May 6	Former CIA Director Casey dies.
June 30	Oliver North turns over documents and personal memos to Senate committees.
July 7	Oliver North begins six days of testimony.
July 14	Robert McFarlane testifies.
July 15	John Poindexter begins five days of testimony.
August 3	Iran-Contra hearings conclude after 250 hours of testimony.
November 18	Iran-Contra Committee issues report.

1988

March 11	McFarlane pleads guilty to withholding information from Congress.
March 16	Federal grand jury indicts North, Poindexter, Secord, Hakim on charges of conspiracy, theft of government property, plus other crimes.
November 8	George Bush elected president.
November 22	Brent Scowcroft named National Security Adviser.

1989

January 5	Lawrence Walsh moves to dismiss government charges against North after White House refuses to supply documents for trial.
January 13	Judge Gerhard A. Gesell dismisses charges against North.
January 20	George Bush inaugurated 41st president.
March 3	McFarlane sentenced to two years probation, fined $20,000.
May 4	North found guilty of destroying NSC documents, aiding and abetting obstruction of Iran-Contra inquiries, and receiving illegal gratuity.
June 3	Ayatollah Ruhollah Khomeini dies.
July 6	North sentenced to 1,200 hours community service, suspended three-year jail sentence, on probation for two years beyond that, fined $150,000. He is characterized as a "low-ranking subordinate."
July 28	Ali Akbar Hashemi Rafsanjani elected president of Iran.
	Lebanese hostage crisis intensifies; Israeli kidnapping of Sheik Abdul Karim Obeid; reported murder of U.S. Lt. Col. William R. Higgins.
September 6	U.S. closes embassy in Beirut.

1990

February 16–17	Reagan gives taped testimony in advance of Poindexter trial.
February 25	Sandinista leader Daniel Ortega voted out of power; Violeta Barrios de Chamorro wins election in Nicaragua.

March 5	Poindexter trial begins.
April 7	Poindexter convicted on five felony charges.
June 11	Poindexter receives prison sentence, first Iran-Contra defendant to face prison.

AMERICAN HOSTAGES IN LEBANON

Name	Position	Date Kidnapped	Status as of October 1990
David Dodge	President, American University of Beirut	July 19, 1982	Released July 20, 1983
Frank Reiger	Department head, American University of Beirut	February 10, 1984	Released April 15, 1984
Jeremy Levin	Bureau chief, Cable News Network	March 7, 1984	Released February 14, 1985
William Buckley	Station chief, Central Intelligence Agency	March 16, 1984	Died June 3, 1985[1]
Benjamin F. Weir	Presbyterian minister	May 8, 1984	Released September 15, 1985
Peter Kilburn	Librarian, American University of Beirut	December 3, 1984	Killed April 14, 1986[2]
Lawrence M. Jenco	Director, Catholic Relief Services	January 8, 1985	Released July 26, 1986
Terry A. Anderson	Chief Middle East correspondent, Associated Press	May 16, 1985	Still held
David P. Jacobsen	Director, American University of Beirut hospital	May 28, 1985	Released November 2, 1986

Name	Position	Date taken	Status
Thomas Sutherland	Acting dean of agriculture, American University of Beirut	June 9, 1985	Still held
Frank H. Reed	Director, Lebanese International School	September 9, 1986	Released April 30, 1990
Joseph J. Cicippio	Acting comptroller, American University of Beirut	September 12, 1986	Still held
Edward A. Tracy	Writer	October 21, 1986	Still held
Alann Steen	Professor, Beirut University College	January 24, 1987	Still held
Jesse J. Turner	Assistant professor, Beirut University College	January 24, 1987	Still held
Robert Polhill	Professor, Beirut University College	January 24, 1987	Released April 22, 1990
Charles Glass	Journalist	June 17, 1987	Escaped August 18, 1987[3]
William Higgins	Lieutenant Colonel	February 1988	Hanged, announced July 31, 1988

[1] Died in captivity probably on this date.
[2] Executed possibly in retaliation for U.S. attack on Libya.
[3] There was some speculation that Glass was allowed to escape.
Source: The Iran-Contra Puzzle, Congressional Quarterly, Inc., 1987.

PHOTOGRAPHY CREDITS

Photographs courtesy of: AP/Wide World Photos: pp. 1 top, 9 top; UPI/Bettmann Newsphotos: pp. 1 bottom, 2, 3 bottom, 4, 5, 7 top left, 7 bottom, 8 bottom, 9 bottom, 10, 11, 12; Gamma-Liaison: pp. 3 top (Hughes Vassal), 16 top (Eslami Rad), 16 bottom (Brad Markel); Reuters/Bettmann Newsphotos: pp. 6, 7 top right, 8 top, 14, 15; Sygma Photo News: p. 13 top (J.L. Atlan); Rothco Cartoons: p. 13 bottom (Wicks).

NOTES

Chapter One
"Nest of Spies"

1. Bernard Gwertzman, "U.S. Rejects Demand of Students in Iran to Send Shah Back," *New York Times*, 6 November, 1979, 2.

Chapter Two
The Rise and Fall of the Shah

1. Amnesty International Report 1977, 296.
2. Howell Raines, "Reagan Hails the Hostages, Vows Action on Any Attack," *New York Times*, 28 January 1981, 14.

Chapter Three
President Reagan Faces a New Hostage Crisis

1. "Reagan Envoy Describes Trip," *New York Times*, 14 November 1986, 9.
2. "Transcript of Remarks by Reagan About Iran," *New York Times*, 14 November, 1986, 8.
3. Barbara Honegger. *October Surprise* (New York: Tudor Publishing Co., 1989), 7.
4. Ibid, 5.
5. Steven V. Roberts, "Panel Said to Hear of Effort to Hide Reagan Iran Role," *New York Times*, 20 February, 1987, 1.

6. Steven V. Roberts, "Reagan Concedes 'Mistake' on Arms-for-Hostage Policy; Takes Blame, Vows Changes," *New York Times*, 5 March, 1987, 1.

Chapter Four
Arms-for-Hostages

1. Bob Schieffer and Gary Paul Gates. *The Acting President* (New York: E.P. Dutton, 1989), 233.
2. Schieffer and Gates, 233.
3. Schieffer and Gates, 269.

Chapter Five
Oliver North and the Iran-Contra Affair

1. Joel Brinkley, "Iran Arms Sales Linked to Broad Covert Program," *New York Times*, 15 February, 1987, 20.
2. Schieffer and Gates, 218.
3. Ibid, 251.

Chapter Six
Operation Damage Control

1. Bernard Weinraub, "Iran Payment Found Diverted to Contras; Reagan Security Adviser and Aide Are Out," *New York Times*, 26 November 1986, 1.
2. Maureen Dowd, "A Fall Guy Yes, a Patsy No, A President's Servant Says," *New York Times*, 10 July, 1987, 1.
3. Congressional Quarterly, *The Iran-Contra Puzzle* (Washington, D.C.: Congressional Quarterly, Inc., 1987), C-87.
4. Testimony by Fawn Hall in *The Iran-Contra Puzzle* (Washington, D.C.: Congressional Quarterly, Inc., 1987), C-63.
5. Excerpts from testimony of Congressional Committee investigating the Iran-Contra Affair: "A Confession: Tearing up a 'Politically Embarrassing' Finding by Reagan . . . Poindexter Continues: Providing Some Future Deniability for the President," *New York Times*, 16 July, 1987, 11.
6. *Taking the Stand: The Testimony of Lieutenant Colonel Oliver L. North* (New York: Pocket Books, 1987), 744–5.
7. *Report of the Congressional Committees Investigating the Iran-Contra Affair* (New York: Random House Inc., 1988), 354.

Chapter Seven
Oliver North and John Poindexter Go to Trial

1. David Rosenbaum, "Jurors See North as a Scapegoat for His Superiors," *New York Times*, 6 May, 1989, 1.
2. David Johnston, "North, Spared Prison, Gets $150,000 Fine and Probation for His Iran-Contra Crimes," *New York Times*, 6 July, 1989, 1.
3. David Johnston, "Poindexter Loses Fight for Reagan Notes," *New York Times*, 22 March 1990, 20.
4. Ibid.
5. Ibid.
6. Material drawn from "Excerpts from Reagan's Testimony on the Iran-Contra Affair," *New York Times*, 23 February, 1990, 18.
7. "Excerpts from Reagan's Testimony on the Iran-Contra Affair," *New York Times*, 23 February, 1990, 18.
8. Drawn from David Johnston, "North Ending Testimony, Speaks Softly and Haltingly of His Lies," *New York Times*, 15 March 1990, 21.
9. David Johnston, "Prosecution Rests in Poindexter Case," *New York Times*, 21 March 1990, 23.
10. David Johnston, "Secret Reports at Trial Hint Congress Knew of Rebel Aid," *New York Times*, 24 March, 1990, 9.
11. David Johnston, "Poindexter Defense Abruptly Rests Case," *New York Times*, 28 March, 1990, 12.
12. David Johnston, "Told to Ignore Policy Questions, Jury Deliberates Poindexter Case," *New York Times*, 3 April 1990, 20.
13. Material in this paragraph drawn from David Johnston, "Iran-Contra Role Brings Poindexter 6 Months in Prison," *New York Times*, 12 June 1990, 1 & 16.
14. David Johnston, "Iran-Contra Panel Opens New Inquiry on Reagan's Aides," *New York Times*, 19 May 1990, 48.

Chapter Eight
President Bush Faces His Own Hostage Crises

1. Quote from Elaine Sciolino, "Washington Talk: Hoax Shows the Limits of Personal Diplomacy," *New York Times*, 13 March 1990. The quote and material used in the rest of the paragraph can also be found in "Headliners," *New York Times*, 11 March 1990, 7.
2. Youssef M. Ibrahim, "Beirut Kidnappers Free American," *New York Times*, 23 April 1990, 1.
3. Ihsan Hijazi, "Iran Reportedly Gave Weapons to Obtain U.S. Hostage Release," *New York Times*, 23 April 1990, 8.

4. Richard Lacayo, "Games Captors Play," *Time*, 30 April 1990, 32.
5. Ibid., 33.
6. Youseff M. Ibrahim, "Militants Promise to Free American," *New York Times*, 19 April 1990. Also, "Hostage Statement Issued by Militants," *New York Times*, 19 April 1990, 8.
7. Thomas L. Friedman, "Militants Delay Hostage Release," *New York Times*, 20 April 1990, 1.
8. Ibid, 2.
9. Thomas L. Friedman, "Bush Denies Any Deal with Iran for Hostage," *New York Times*, 23 April 1990, 8.
10. Drawn from Ihsan A. Hijazi, "Beirut Captors Say They Will Free Second American," *New York Times*, 30 April 1990, B8.
11. Andrew Rosenthal, "Second American Freed in Lebanon," *New York Times*, 1 May 1990, 12.
12. "U.S. Informs Iran on $ Missing in Lebanon," *New York Times*, 30 May 1990, 3.
13. Thomas L. Friedman, "For Captors, Less in Common Now with Iran?" *New York Times*, 24 April 1990. Also, George J. Church, "One Home, 21 to Go," *Time*, 7 May 1990, 40–42.

BIBLIOGRAPHY

Bill, James A. *The Eagle and the Lion*. New Haven: Yale University Press, 1988.
Bradlee, Ben, Jr. *Guts and Glory—The Rise and Fall of Oliver North*. New York: Donald L. Fine, Inc., 1988.
Church, George J. "One Home, 21 to Go," *Time*, 7 May 1990, 40–42.

Cockburn, Leslie. *Out of Control.* New York: Atlantic Monthly Press, 1987.

Cohen, William S. and George J. Mitchell. *Men of Zeal: A Candid Inside Story of the Iran-Contra Hearings.* New York: Viking Penguin Inc., 1988.

Congressional Quarterly, *The Iran-Contra Puzzle.* Washington, D.C.: Congressional Quarterly, Inc., 1987.

Glass, Charles. *Tribes with Flags: A Dangerous Passage through the Chaos of the Middle East.* New York: Atlantic Monthly Press, 1989.

Hersh, Seymour H. "The Iran-Contra Committees. Did They Protect Reagan?" *New York Times Magazine,* 29 April 1990, 47ff.

Honegger, Barbara. *October Surprise.* New York: Tudor Publishing Co., 1989.

Lacayo, Richard. "Games Captors Play," *Time,* 30 April 1990, 32–33.

Lawson, Don. *Ronald Reagan, the Picture Life.* New York: Franklin Watts, 1985.

Manchester, William. *The Glory and the Dream.* New York: Bantam Books, 1975. (P)

Mayer, Jane and Doyle McManus. *Landslide: The Unmaking of the President, 1984–1988.* Boston: Houghton Mifflin, 1988.

Moyers, Bill. "The Secret Government . . . The Constitution in Crisis," Public Affairs TV, *Transcript Journal Graphics.* New York: Alvin H. Perlmutter, Inc. 1987. (P)

The New York Times.

Schieffer, Bob and Gary Paul Gates. *The Acting President.* New York: E. P. Dutton, 1989.

Taheri, Amir. *Nest of Spies.* New York: Pantheon Books, 1988.

Taking the Stand. The Testimony of Lieutenant Colonel Oliver North. New York: Pocket Books, 1987. (P)

Whitney, David C. *The American Presidents.* Garden City: Doubleday & Co., 1967.

INDEX